Published by

kp *fw*

Krause Publications, a division of F+W Media, Inc.
700 East State Street • Iola, WI 54990-0001
715-445-2214 • 888-457-2873
www.krausebooks.com

To order books or other products call toll-free 1-800-258-0929
or visit us online at www.krausebooks.com

Front cover photography by Kris Kandler. Back cover: Heer soldier; three-place civilian mounted
medal bar with iron cross, Hindenburg, and social welfare medals, $300-$375 (Private Collection);
political leader shirt, tie, and armband, $700-$800; political leader gorget, $1,000-$1,200; eagle and
cockade from enlisted sailor's "Donald Duck"-style cap, $75-$85; DLV chain-stitched insignia from
a flag center, $75-$125; variant Allgemeine SS guard's helmet, $1,800-$2,500.

ISBN-13: 978-1-4402-4448-3
ISBN-10: 1-4402-4448-0

Cover Design by Kevin Ulrich
Designed by Kevin Ulrich
Edited by Mary Sieber

10 9 8 7 6 5 4 3 2 1

Contents

OPPOSITE: Overview of the mass roll call of SA, SS, and NSKK troops.
Nuremberg, Nov. 9, 1935. UNITED STATES NATIONAL ARCHIVES: Charles Russell, Photographer

Acknowledgments

Since I first began collecting items of the Third Reich, the quest to discover that next item and then share each new find with good friends in the hobby has been an ongoing source of enjoyment, and a renewing catalyst for my continuing study of history. I have met a number of fine fellow hobbyists and dealers who were willing to share their knowledge of this extensive and diverse subject matter. I have also had the pleasure of knowing many ordinary German World War II combatants and civilians, and find most were truly devoted to what they were led to believe was best for their country at the time. Collecting memorabilia has developed a true bridge between our present day and the places and events of the past that helped form the times we live in now. By studying the Third Reich in particular, one can see how blind obedience to a charismatic leader can quickly lead a traditional and moral society to ultimate destruction.

I thank my wife, Lisa, and my daughter, Maria, for their patience during all the unplanned stops at antique stores, estate sales, and homes of veterans, for forgiving my many weekend absences to attend shows, and for their continued support throughout the hundreds of hours I needed to put this book together.

I owe special debts of gratitude to my brother, Bob, for cultivating my early interest in militaria and firearms, and to Leroy Kile, my mentor in the hobby for over 25 years, who has always shared his vast knowledge whenever I asked.

My great friends Chris Depere and Rick Fleury are always a tremendous help in providing items to photograph and being soundboards for my prose.

And I thank John Adams-Graf for his encouragement, the sharing of his experience, and allowing me access to his wonderful photo library.

Introduction

After Adolf Hitler led a group of fanatical nationalists to political victory in the German Weimar Republic, he began to build his ideal new empire, which became known as the Thousand Year Reich. However, history would remember the new leader and his subsequent accomplishments much differently than his followers had first envisioned. No other man of the 20th century can summon more fear, loathing, and contempt within our current Western culture.

Though coming from humble beginnings, Hitler rose to be the driving force behind the deaths and exploitation of millions of people, including countless citizens of his own adopted country. Yet despite this, artifacts of the Third Reich are accumulated by today's collectors and military buffs who appreciate each piece for its artistic beauty and attention to design, rather than the abhorrent acts of the regime that created them.

Adolf Hitler was born on April 20,1889 to 52-year-old Alois and 29-year-old Klara Hitler in the village of Braunau am inn, Austria. When Adolf was six years old, his father, a civil servant, retired and moved the family to the small village of Hafeld, Austria. A favorite of his doting mother but a disappointment to his dominating father, Hitler spent an unremarkable childhood in the small Austrian town. He attended the nearby Fischlam school where he did well academically, but had numerous disciplinary problems due to his disrespect for authority. After his father's sudden demise from heart disease, Hitler left the family home to pursue studies in painting and architecture funded by his

meager inheritance and help from his mother. With her early death from cancer in 1907, the 18-year-old student was left without means, eventually living on the streets of Vienna for three years and sleeping at a vagrant's hostel.

Unemployed most of the time, Hitler produced and sold his small watercolor paintings and postcards to eke out a subsistence living. With Germany's entry into World War I in 1914, 25-year-old Hitler immediately enlisted in the German Army and served with distinction (he was awarded the iron cross 1st class and 3rd class wound badge) as an enlisted courier. At the end of the war, Hitler, temporarily blinded by an allied gas attack, began to formulate his hatred for the leaders of Germany while he convalesced and spoke with his

fellow soldiers about the injustices of their defeat. The occupation of his beloved Fatherland by Allied forces, loss of German territories, and Germany's heavy economic reparation toll under the Treaty of Versailles would later grow this abhorrence to even greater heights.

Upon being released from medical care in 1919, Hitler began a new career in the *Reichswehr* (post-war army) intelligence corps, with his first assignment being the infiltration of the *Deutsche Arbeiterpartei* (DAP, German workers party), one of the many radical right-wing factions battling for power in the chaotic streets of the Allied-sanctioned Weimar Republic. Once introduced to the group, Hitler avidly agreed with their core beliefs of nationalism, anti-Semitism and "Aryan" superiority, joining as member 555 (number 55; the group added 500 to make its membership appear larger). He was immediately recognized for his unique oratory skills, which made him a natural public speaker. By 1921, through a series of political intrigues, he became the chairman of the DAP and eventually changed its name to the *Nationalsozialistische Deutsche Arbeiterpartei* (National Socialist German Workers Party – NSDAP – Nazi).

Being in a constant conflict with other parties for public support, the group's main adversaries were the members of the Communist Party along with the Social Democrats. In the early meetings, Communists regularly broke into the Nazi auditoriums or beer halls (and inversely, Nazis disrupted the Communist gatherings), so Hitler formed a protective group, the *Sturmabteilung* (SA, or storm troopers) to guard its members, keep order in the meetings, throw the agitators out, and attack attendees at Communist meetings. When political battles became more physical, the SA fought the Communists with their fists, clubs and pistols in the cities and villages across the country. In addition, the SA punished others who did not support them or those they viewed as non-German undesirables.

In 1923 Hitler headed an attempted failure to overthrow the government through his Beer Hall Putsch, the result of which left 16 Nazis dead from police bullets and Hitler sentenced to prison for treason. While in Landsberg prison, Hitler wrote his autobiography and the outline for his plans of world domination, *Mein Kampf* (*My Struggle*), which became mandatory reading for all members of the party. After his release, the Nazis continued their struggle for national prominence by street brawling, holding numerous meetings, conducting propaganda campaigns, and providing food and winter fuel for the German poor during the post-war depression. By these persistent efforts the party was able to attract more and more active members and casual followers.

Volksgemeinschaft (a German concept of "people's community," which eliminated class boundaries in order to bind the people together as one ethnic unit) was actively promoted by the Nazis in their public speeches. In addition, Nazi rhetoric included strict nationalism, ethnic/racial pride, a call for the re-emergence of the past great German empire, active rebellion against the perceived unfair Treaty of Versailles, and blame for most problems placed on the heads of the ever-present scapegoats: gypsies, homosexuals, Freemasons and, above all, Jews.

Hitler targeted the Jewish population by escalating age-old discriminatory practices and pogroms (systematic massacres of ethnic Jews) that had resurfaced from time to time across Europe since the 14th century. With the combination of stringent war reparations and the early advent of the great world depression hitting Germany harder than most other countries (under the shadow of reparations with many of their major industries seized), Hitler and the Nazis were able to feed the German people, who were starving for both bread and a feeling of self-worth. Medals, ribbons, badges and other awards were handed out by the Nazis to thousands of people in all walks of life to build their self-esteem and feeling of community spirit.

In January 1933, Hitler, though short of overall votes to be democratically elected as the leader of Germany, convinced politicians around the aging president, General Field Marshal Paul Von Hindenburg, to have himself appointed chancellor so that he and his riotous group could be better controlled by the same politicians. At the end of February 1933, the Nazis burned down the *Reichstag* (parliament building), blamed it on a Jew, and declared martial law with the blessings of the German government. With Von Hindenburg's death from old age in August 1934, Hitler was now proclaimed the leader of Germany, declaring himself the *Fuhrer* (leader) of *Das Dritte Reich* (the Third Reich).

Hitler had learned early on that complete control

of every citizen in the country must be maintained, thus giving him the ability to have any and all of his policies carried out without question. Life for the average citizen in Hitler's Germany meant voluntary or involuntary involvement in a series of political, professional, social, paramilitary, and military groups. It was not unusual for much of a person's free time to be spent in small meetings, mass gatherings, and events where they fulfilled their commitments to participate under the watchful eyes of their fellow citizens. As only one political group existed, State-directed meetings for

political leaders and citizenry as a whole were meant to reinforce the doctrines of NSDAP beliefs by those members being fed a constant diet of Nazi dogma. All major and minor achievements were touted as benefits from the party's leadership roles with the Fuhrer as the main architect. If a person was a teacher, doctor, accountant, or other professional, joining the Nazi Party (there were 8.5 million members by the end of the war) was a must to maintain and elevate one's career.

Social groups tended to revolve around the ideals of the Party, with emphasis leaning toward participation in athletic and sporting events to physically and mentally harden the individuals, build team spirit, and identify natural leaders. Paramilitary groups (highly organized civilian groups based on a military format

but not considered parts of an actual military unit) were especially abundant in the Third Reich as much of Hitler's agenda of *Lebensraum* – the expansion of the Reich and its citizens at the expense of "inferior" people – called for a large-scale military buildup for future conquests and expansion.

The Treaty of Versailles had limited the German armed forces to just 100,000 men in direct conflict with Hitler's quest for a large armed force. To circumvent this, many of the paramilitary organizations were formed as clandestine instruction grounds for their members to shorten their training time when they were inducted into an actual military branch. As the rearmament programs escalated under Hitler's guidance, the SA moved from an organization of meeting guards and street ruffians to a full-fledged pre-military organization. Many of the other paramilitary groups followed later by readying their members for the rigors of future military service.

Joining the *Wehrmacht* (armed forces) was considered the ultimate service to the country in Hitler's Reich. Throughout many of his public speeches and private comments, Hitler held military duty and sacrifice for the *Volk* (German people) as a young German's most praiseworthy attribute. The armed forces went from a total of 100,000 members in 1920 to over 17.9 million serving throughout World War II. The Wermacht included the *Heer* (army), *Kriegsmarine* (navy), *Luftwaffe* (air force), and the *Waffen Schutzstaffel* (armed SS). The government spared no expense in supplying soldiers and their support personnel with the best and smartest uniforms, equipment, and weaponry that they could acquire. However, when raw materials and manpower became meager as the war progressed, quality fell off in fit and finish. As is a contradiction in the whole of German society, the military sought out the new while maintaining the old: the newest technology available, while at the same time strictly adhering to many aspects of the traditional military cultures. With mandatory conscription put in place, many German soldiers fought long and valiantly on all fronts, though they may or may not have believed in the ideals of the Nazi regime.

Despite their overwhelming victories in 1939 and 1940, Hitler's refusal to work with his seasoned general

staff, his misunderstanding of the determination and fighting ability of the Allies, and the impossible logistics of running a war along the thousands of battlefield line miles spelled the evidential doom for the armed forces of Nazi Germany. The defeat of the Third Reich was never more historically justified than when public disclosure surfaced at the end of the war revealing the multiple killing camps erected for mass extermination as well as numerous other atrocities committed by the Nazi regime and its followers. When the war ended and Hitler lay dead by his own hand, most Germans, tired of war and no longer believing in their government, wanted to distance themselves from the trappings of the Reich. They freely discarded many of their political, paramilitary, and military items. To further expedite this process, retention of Nazi-themed items by German citizens became illegal, with harsh punishments dealt out by the Allied occupying forces.

Collecting German war trophies became commonplace among the Allied soldiers as each victory in Europe brought them closer to the heart of the dying Reich. British, Russian, American and other Allies practiced the age-old custom of taking souvenirs as reminders of their wartime conquests. These items were kept not to glorify their enemies, but to demonstrate their own prowess as conquerors and to show appreciation for the items' intrinsic values. Beautifully crafted daggers, elaborate swords, well-made firearms, tailored uniforms and caps, along with colorful medals and badges were packed away and mailed home. German citizens were ordered to surrender all their former Nazi materials, which were often collected at central city or village drop-off sites. Here, battle weary and bored GIs sorted through piles of relics and shipped home those items that appealed to them the most, leaving the rest to be burned or buried.

Though a limited amount of insignia was retained by their former owners in Germany, most surviving items found their way into the dresser drawers, attics,

and basements of American and other Allied soldiers' homes. Just as conquering GIs appreciated Nazi regalia in 1945, today's collectors value these same items as mementos of a soldier's valor as well as for the creative design and psychological thought behind each piece. Because of similarities between paramilitary and military groups within the Third Reich, items from both are held in high regard by collectors and are highly sought after.

Values are based on three criteria: condition, rarity, and provenance (an item documented to a well-known personality). A Knights Cross to the Iron Cross in nearly any condition, because of rarity, will generally be worth more than a 1st class iron cross in excellent condition. When provenance is thrown into play, the other factors in determining value become secondary, and the history carries the value of the piece. The craftsmanship (accounting for available materials and expertise), artistic merit, and calculated thought (awards were developed to instill individual pride and national unity) behind the production of an item are apparent once a collector studies each new find in detail.

Additionally, to understand the significance of why certain objects appear as they do, it is important to have an understanding of the various groups, their backgrounds and the functions they performed during their existence. Knowing these things can help a collector determine which group an item may have originated from, who received it, and how it was displayed or used. With the profuse number of organizations in Hitler's Germany, this can sometimes seem a daunting task. But with diligent study of these groups and item descriptions, a collector can learn to distinguish the differences in artifacts, and more fully enjoy a hobby where new knowledge of history truly becomes its own reward.

Good hunting!
Chris William

Sturmabteilung (SA)

During the early years of the Nazi party's struggle to gain prominence in the political arena, Adolf Hitler found it necessary to have a small group of toughened guards protect him and other speakers during meetings and rallies. The first *Sallschutz Abteilung* (hall defense detachment) was formularized into the *Sturmabteilung* (SA, storm detachment) in September 1921, becoming the official guard unit of Hitler and the eventual private army of the Nazi party.

The membership grew steadily as large numbers of unemployed veterans joined the SA in order to regain the camaraderie they had lost after leaving the military, developed networking channels to find work, and in dire circumstances received help with basic food and shelter needs. The first duties of the SA as meeting guards later expanded into police assistants, major participants in mass demonstrations, streetside fund collectors, campaigners (prior to Hitler's election in 1933), street brawlers attacking non-German antagonists, and brutal concentration camp guards. The exponential growth of this group was due in part to the leadership of former army Capt. Ernst Rohm, a flamboyant war hero. However, Hitler's jealousy of Rohm's power and general paranoia brought on by intrigue within the party leadership from Joseph Goebbels, Heinrich Himmler, and Herman Goering led to Rohm's murder in 1934, along with 200 other high-ranking SA leaders at the hands of the *Schutzstaffel* (SS – protection squadron) during the *Nacht der langen Messer* (night of the long knives). After this lethal change, the SA's power was diminished, though it still remained a large and dominant organization until the end of the war.

The organization was divided into 21 *Gruppen* (sections) – 29 after the addition of the new territories – that covered all of Greater Germany and which were broken down further into Brigade, Standarten, Sturmbanne, and Sturme. As neighboring countries were occupied, new SA units were established among each country's residents. The hierarchy of members began with the Oberster SA-Fuhrer, and then went to Gruppenfuhrer, Oberfuhrer, Standartenfuhrer, Sturmbahnfuhrer, Sturmhauptfuhrer, Sturmfuhrer, Truppfuhrer, Scharfuhrer, and Mann. Besides the standard SA organizations, in 1939 the *Wehrmannschaft* (SA reserve) groups were formed from the older members as an auxiliary paramilitary group to assist the SA in times when supplementary manpower was needed. In addition, the SA always maintained a close relationship with the Hitler Youth, as the *Jungendbund* (early Nazi youth members) who had become the nucleus of the HJ formations were originally led by SA members until becoming a separate organization in 1932.

The first SA uniforms were a haphazard lot that generally consisted of gray/tan windbreakers, matching riding pants, boots, and soft tan visor caps. The NSDAP armband and party membership pins were the only significant additions that identified the wearer as an SA man. In 1926 a large quantity of surplus World War I army tropical shirts were purchased by the party for distribution to the SA members so that some uniformity of attire could be established among the members. These brown shirts, which became the SA nickname and basis for future organizational color designations, were worn with a tie, riding pants or lederhosen, white high socks, and boots or shoes. The shirt collars had attached collar boards with different colors, numbers, stripes, pips and piping to designate the SA group, unit and rank of the wearer. Shoulder boards were color-coordinated with the collar tabs and further designated rank. A standard NSDAP armband consisting of a black rotated swastika on a white circle over a red band was worn between the shoulder and elbow on the left arm. Military and political awards that the wearer had earned were proudly worn in their respective places on either the left or right front panels of the uniform. Among these awards was likely to be an SA sports award. These were earned by the recipients for participating in an SA-sponsored ongoing testing process of physical abilities and political indoctrination. Awards were in the design of a 57mm upturned sword surrounded by an oak leaf wreath over a canted swastika. They were awarded in bronze, silver and gold, with subsidiary designs issued for war wounded and SA Marine units. Since the SA was an NSDAP-sanctioned organization, members wore their round enamel party pins on either the left front breast pocket of their shirts or on the front of their neckties.

Overcoats of brown-colored wool were worn in inclement weather while a formal four-pocket jacket was developed in 1932 for daily wear by administrative officials. A rectangular belt buckle of gilded brass – with a half-circle of oak leaves cradling an eagle with outstretched wings perched on either a static or rotating oak leaf-encircled swastika – was worn on a brown leather belt with cross strap. From these belts were suspended some of the most uniquely designed daggers attributed to the Third Reich. Modeled after a 16th century Swiss hunting knife, the SA dagger consisted of a long double-sided blade with *Alles für Deutschland* (everything for Germany) acid etched along the center section. A maker's mark or later *Reichs zeugmeisterei* (RZM, national material control office) code or both were

engraved on the blade ricasso. The hourglass-shaped wooden handle was mounted on either end by German silver or nickel-plated crosspieces, an inlet with an eagle over swastika, and a round SA emblem in enamel set above. The dagger was carried in an anodized (type of metal bluing process) or later brown-painted scabbard suspended from a leather strap and metal clip. Daggers could be custom-ordered with dedicative inscriptions, Damascus steel blades, or other embellishments such as carved handles or leather-covered scabbards. Although rarely seen, the SA did occasionally use a dress sword while on parade, which consisted of a D-handled model with a plain nickel pommel, back strap, cross guard, and silver wire-wrapped black celluloid handle. The nickel-plated blade was etched with *Alles für Deutschland* in gold along the center panel length. Headwear consisted of a rounded visor cap ("coffee can," first soft, then hard material construction) with leather chinstrap and

upper half colored top that matched the colors of the unit collar tabs. The cap front bore a finished button and party eagle in silver perched on a rotated swastika in an oak leaf circle. Though not always recognized as official badges, many SA men wore tinnies or traditions badges (items traditionally identified with one group or important event) on the sides of their caps.

Each SA member was issued an *SA Ausweis* (membership identity book). This book was produced in an oilcloth material with the recipient's photo stapled to the inside cover. Personal information such as name, address, occupation, and birthdate were included. Places were allotted for entrance date into the SA, NSDAP party number, and signature of the local unit commander.

While in civilian attire, SA men wore a silver lapel membership pin of a circle with a stylized "SA" in the center.

When SA men participated in sporting events, they wore an SA patch on their field sports shirts. These patches consisted of either a short winged eagle clutching an oak leaf wreath with canted swastika in black on a white background, or a stylized "SA" in a circle color-coordinated to match their respective SA group.

Reservist members of the Wehrmannschaft wore uniforms similar to those of the SA four-pocket tunics but darker green in color. They bore armbands of a golden brown wreath surrounding an upturned sword and swastika on a white circle over red background. (These were later changed to the standard NSDAP armband in 1942). Caps consisted of an Italian-style overseas cap in the matching green materials. When in civilian clothing, reservists wore a membership pin of a silver canted swastika on a white shield supported by two outstretched silver wings. Each member was issued an *ausweis* (identification document) that included his name, address, and other required information.

The SA remained an active part of the Nazi party until Germany's surrender at which time it was disbanded in May 1945.

SA Ostmark kepi. **$1,500-$1,900**

(JAG)

SA Obertruppfuhrer wool overcoat with armband. **$700-$850**

SA collar tab, Westmark, 15th Sturm, 27th Standarte. **$140-$175**

(Private Collection)

SA honor chevron. **$50-$75**

(Private Collection)

SA Edelweiss embroidered cap badge. **$125-$150**

SA Obersturmfuhrer Schlesien collar tab. **$100-$125**

SA sports badge embroidered cloth sports vest insignia. **$175-$250**

SA early sports vest eagle. **$125-$150**

SA crewmember flyer's bullion wing. **$450-$575**

SA pilot's wing in bullion. **$550-$675**

(Rick Fleury by JAG)

SA Wehrmannschaft reservist armband. **$175-$250**

SA small belt buckle. **$90-$150**

(Private Collection)

SA mobile (sun wheel) swastika silver-plate on brass belt buckle. **$200-$275**

SA mobile swastika all-brass belt buckle. **$175-$200**

SA canted swastika brass belt buckle. **$175-$200**

SA model 1933 dagger, maker-marked with hanging strap. **$525-$950**

SA marked leather medical case. **$225-$275**

SA command center pennant. **$350-$425**

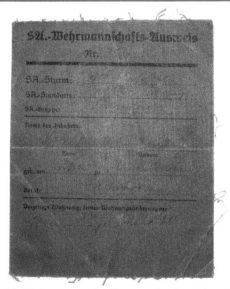

SA Wehrmannschaft ausweis. **$100-$150**

SA membership ausweis. **$200-$275**

SA reservist ausweis. **$75-$100**

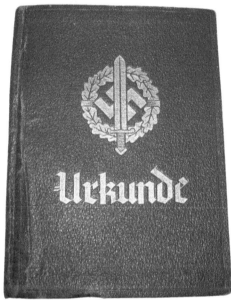

SA sports badge award booklet to a young HJ man. **$225-$275**

SA sports badge training manual. **$125-$150**

SA table medal for second-place sports event winner. **$250-$300**

SA sports badge for war wounded. **$350-$475**

SA bronze sports badge. **$85-$125**

SA gold sports badge. **$250-$300**

SA silver sports badge. **$150-$200**

Gau Essen traditions badge. **$250-$350**

SA sports award in zinc for war wounded. **$300-$400**

SA candid photos. **$10-$15 each**

Gau Munich traditions badge. **$275-$350**

SA Treffen Braunschweig traditions badge, solid back RZM. **$275-$350**

(Rick Fleury)

SA reservist member stickpin. **$50-$85**

SA gold sports badge stickpin. **$75-$125**

SA membership stickpin. **$85-$100**

SA pinback. **$40-$50**

(Rick Fleury)

1934 SA/SS ski competitor's badge. **$450-$500**

Early SA/NSKK crash helmet eagle insignia. **$175-$200**

SA flyer collar tab insignia. **$175-$225**

(Rick Fleury by JAG)

SA shield tinnie, heavy metal with pinback. **$125-$150**

(Rick Fleury)

SA 1937 Dortmund tinnie. **$75-$95**

(Rick Fleury)

Early SA cap eagle with prongs. **$85-$100**

SA 1934 Stuttgart meeting tinnie. **$125-$150**

SA 1938 Dortmund meeting plastic tinnie. **$75-$85**

SA 1939 Bavarian meeting porcelain tinnie. **$125-$150**

SA-style desktop ornament, light metal with plating. **$45-$55**

(Rick Fleury)

SA 1937 Niederrhein pressed tin tinnie. **$150-$175**

SA 1939 Nordsee plastic tinnie. **$75-$85**

(Private Collection)

SA 1939 Hochland meeting tinnie. **$150-$185**

NSDAP
Politischer Leiter

When the membership in the fledgling NSDAP grew large enough, it was deemed necessary to form an official political hierarchy spanning the German countryside. This newly found heart of the Nazi party became the instrument that channeled the core beliefs and the ever-changing orders from the top of Hitler's dictatorship down to the common people, while at the same time keeping the nation's citizens under constant observation and tightening controls. As a highly visible and dedicated group, the NSDAP *Politische Leitung* (Nazi Political Leader Organization) helped Hitler secure and maintain the civic functions of the German nation.

In 1930 the political leaders were formally organized in order to more efficiently feed a constant stream of propaganda to the German people about the benefits of national Socialism, the evils of communism and democracy, anti-Semitism, and to help increase the membership of the growing Nazi party. During the national elections of 1931 to 1933, political leaders were instrumental in election campaigning, securing votes through any means possible, polling the populace to monitor potential outcomes, and reporting back to Hitler's political committees. With the Nazi's ascension to power in 1933, the political leader network was exponentially expanded so that it could operate in conjunction with (and eventually replace) existing municipal and national workforce leaderships. Many city and state officials found it advantageous to become part of the NSDAP leadership program, which gave them increased political clout, power and acceptance. But by doing so,

this allowed the Nazi party to establish a more secure network to control the daily business of the government and its citizens.

The Political Leadership Organization was divided into four main administrative branches beginning with the lowest, *Ortsgruppen* (local towns, villages and neighborhoods), followed by groups of leaders appointed through Hitler consisting of *Kriesleitung* (county, numbering 920 Kriese), *Gauleitung* (district, numbering 43 Gaue) and *Reichleitung* (national or state). Many of Hitler's old comrades from their "period of struggle" were awarded appointments in the top tiers of the political leader structure once he came to power. Ranking within these groups went through a series of changes from 1930 to 1939, with the last system consisting of 28 different ranks shared within the four levels.

Uniforms worn by political leaders went through a number of transformations from 1930 until their final accepted forms in 1939. Members at all levels were required to purchase their own uniforms. Because Germany was in the depths of a deep economic and political depression, many of the leaders, especially those of the lower ranks, were unable to afford the authorized uniforms and carried out their duties while wearing civilian clothing.

The basic uniform consisted of a heavy, light brown long-sleeved shirt with five gilded front buttons decorated with eagles clutching swastikas over a pebbled background, with back-to-back matching conjoint button closures on each cuff. Shirts without insignia were worn in the beginning years, but the level of leadership was eventually designated by colored piping around the collar base (by 1939, light blue piping designated Ortsgruppen, white Kriesleitung, red Gauleitung, and gold Reichleitung). Elongated rectangular patches were worn on collars with a series of colors, swastika-embossed bullion tapes, metal or embroidered bars, piping, eagles, pips, and oak leaves to indicate one of the 28 ranks ranging from *Anwarter* (candidate) to *Reichsleiter* (Reich Leader). The collar was closed with a black or later golden brown tie. Fastened to the left front pocket was the round NSDAP membership pin of black canted enamel swastika on a white circle surrounded by a red border supporting the phrase "Nationalsozialiste DAP" along the edge. Military or civilian awards (such as a 1st class iron cross or NSDAP service awards) were worn on their respective places attached to the left or right front shirt panels. Tan riding pants, black boots and brown leather belt with or without a matching cross strap and gilded buckle were worn.

Buckles were either rectangular with a pebbled finish and two separate swivel posts (double claw) or the more ornate round gilded buckle with a stretch-winged eagle over a canted swastika surrounded by an oak leaf border. The round buckle was attached to a gilded

oak leaf-embellished belt loop on one side, while a mirror image keeper on the tongue end of the belt was secured to the buckle with a hook on the reverse. If a small caliber pistol was authorized for wear, it was often carried in a well-made flap holster of light brown leather with an outstretched eagle perched on an oak leaf-surrounded swastika embossed on the flap (or an eagle made of stamped metal), and sometimes suspended with a double eagle, swastika and oak leaf-ornamented hanger of gilded metal mounted on the top reverse.

Armbands were an important part of the political leaders' attire and changed significantly over time, beginning with the standard NSDAP armband of black swastika on a white circle mounted on a red field, to increasingly elaborate combinations including white tapes, golden oak leaf bands, color-coordinated or bullion oak leaf borders (matching the wearer's level), and gilded pips with raised eagles and swastikas.

A light brown, wide-lapelled four-button tunic with

gilded eagle buttons was introduced for ceremonial and administrative office wear. This was worn over a white or tan shirt with a golden brown tie, black trousers and black shoes, or tan riding pants and black boots. A gold leaf bullion and brown-striped brocade belt and cross strap accented uniforms for parades and other formal occasions. White tunics were introduced for use in the summer months and were coupled with either white straight-leg or brown riding pants. A long, double-breasted golden brown 10-button wool coat protected the leader in inclement weather. These bore the owner's rank tabs on the collars and were worn with or without a large brown leather belt and gilded buckle around the outer waist.

Uniforms were topped off with peaked caps consisting of high-quality light brown bodies (white for summer) with dark brown headbands, appropriate level piping, patent leather brown visors, and gold bullion chinstraps. The front insignia took the form of a gilded, horizontally elongated oak leaf wreath surrounding a red enameled roundel with a black swastika at its center. Above this rested a golden national eagle with outstretched wings perched on a round wreath with canted swastika.

Due to the shortage of adequate supplies and confusion over changing or misinterpreted regulations, many uniformed members did not always show consistency in their attire, combining unauthorized older and newer insignias and even items from other NSDAP groups. In addition, because of personal preferences, many top Nazis (such as Dr. Joseph Goebbels, propaganda minister) wore no insignia at all on their tunic lapels. However, when political leaders were in full official parade dress with their lavishly well-tailored uniforms, brocade belts, armbands and headgear, many fellow Germans secretly referred to them as "Golden Peacocks."

Despite the grand appearance of political leaders, their main business was to promote the NSDAP philosophy and carry out the brutal orders of Hitler's dictatorship. With the defeat of the Nazi regime in 1945, the political leader group was declared a criminal organization and immediately disbanded by the occupying Allies, with many higher-ranking members tried for war crimes against humanity.

NSDAP political leader Ortsgruppe visor cap.
$650-$900

Political leader shirt, tie, and armband. **$700-$800**

Political leader gorget. **$1,000-$1,200**

Political leader Ortsgruppe tunic, pants, and cap.
$3,800-$4,500

(JAG)

Political leader riding pants. **$375-$450**

Political leader, section leader collar tab. **$185-$250**

(Private Collection)

Political leader Ortsgruppe collar tabs. **$100-$125**

(Private Collection)

Political leader collar tabs, head subdivision leader. **$250-$325**

NSDAP political leader belt and buckle. **$375-$450**

Political leader belt buckle. **$250-$285**

(Rick Fluery by JAG)

NSDAP membership sleeve shield. **$200-$250**

Small printed NSDAP armband. **$75-$100**

NSADP standard bevo machine-embroidered armband. **$135-$175**

NSDAP funeral wreath sash, 5 ft. long. **$125-$175**

NSDAP membership book. **$475-$750**

Political leader armband, Ortsgruppenleiter.
$550-$625

(Rick Fluery by JAG)

Political leader ausweis. **$250-$300**

(Rick Fluery by JAG)

NSDAP three-piece sewn standard party armband.
$125-$175

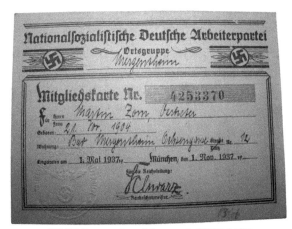

NSDAP membership card. **$125-$150**

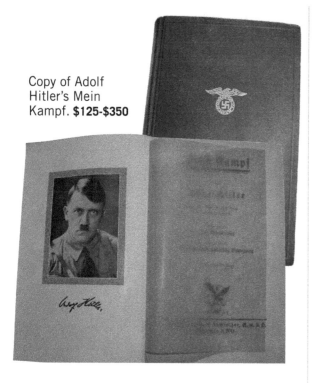

Copy of Adolf Hitler's Mein Kampf. **$125-$350**

Adolf Hitler Bruckner formal pattern dinner spoon. **$1,500-$1,750**

Adolf Hitler Bruckner formal pattern dinner fork. **$1,500-$1,750**

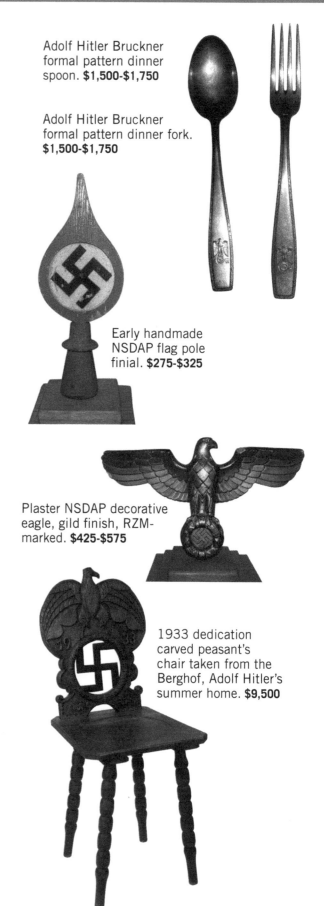

Early handmade NSDAP flag pole finial. **$275-$325**

Plaster NSDAP decorative eagle, gild finish, RZM-marked. **$425-$575**

1933 dedication carved peasant's chair taken from the Berghof, Adolf Hitler's summer home. **$9,500**

Adolf Hitler color postcard. **$50-$85**

Early 1934 NSDAP political postcard. **$45-$65**

NSDAP political 2-1/2" x 4" decorative eagle. **$85-$125**

NSDAP building eagle, RZM on reverse. **$650-$900**

State Service flag, 5 ft. x 8 ft. **$350-$400**

Standard NSDAP party flag, 2 ft. x 4 ft. **$150-$200**

NSDAP party parade flag, 4" x 12". **$65-$85**

NSDAP two-sided banner or flag, 3 ft. x 7 ft. **$225-$275**

NSDAP paper and candle party lantern. **$125-$175**

Tri-color parade flag, 7" x 12". **$45-$60**

Tri-color paper parade flag on stick. **$35-$50**

NSDAP podium banner with fringe, 2-1/2 ft. x 2-1/2 ft. **$275-$350**

Early Ortsgruppe standard flag, 4 ft. x 4 ft. **$475-$650**

NSDAP wall banner with white tape, 4 ft. x 4 ft. **$275-$350**

NSDAP street banner, 3-1/2 ft. x 11 ft. **$250-$300**

NSDAP podium banner with fringe and tape, 2-1/2 ft. x 2-1/2 ft. **$275-$350**

Political leader podium banner, silver thread on red cloth, 2-1/2 ft. x 2-1/2 ft. **$450-$600**

NSDAP long pennant, 1-1/2 ft. x 10 ft. **$250-$300**

Tri-color and swastika pennant, 5" x 10". **$75-$90**

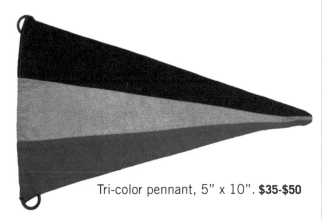

Tri-color pennant, 5" x 10". **$35-$50**

Handmade NSDAP party pennant, 6" x 10". **$75-$100**

NSDAP three-piece party pennants, 4" x 8", on string. **$125-$175**

High-quality multi-piece sewn party hanging pennant with tassel, 4" x 16". **$135-$175**

Set of 10 paper NSDAP pennants on string. **$150-$175**

Political leader wall tapestry, 6 ft. x 9 ft. **$6,500-$8,500**

1939 model political cap eagle.
$120-$150

Political cap eagle in silver.
$75-$95

NSDAP membership eagle pin.
$85-$135

NSDAP patriotic watch fob.
$150-$200

Silver political supporter medal.
$175-$250

(Private Collection)

Bronze boxed Hitler supporter
table medal. **$250-$325**

(Private Collection)

Silver boxed Hitler supporter
table medal. **$250-$325**

(Private Collection)

NSDAP war service medal.
$45-$65

Saar annexation tinnie. **$100-$125**

(Private Collection)

Political leader buttons. **$20-$35**

NSDAP enamel membership
pin. **$85-$125**

Political leader enamel cap roundel. **$50-$75**

NSDAP small party membership badge. **$185-$225**

NSDAP honor membership badge. **$1,500-$1,800**

(JAG)

NSDAP small party affiliate enamel badge. **$95-$145**

Variant NSDAP enamel membership necklace badge (jeweler modified). **$200-$275**

Hungarian Nazi party enamel badge. **$135-$175**

NSDAP painted membership badge. **$75-$95**

NSDAP late version national eagle stickpin. **$100-$125**

Silver-plated static swastika stickpin. **$65-$85**

"Nun Erst Recht" political support enamel badge. **$135-$165**

Westmark political support enamel badge. **$95-$125**

NSDAP early version national eagle stickpin. **$100-$125**

Variant NSDAP lithograph stickpin. **$95-$145**

"Deutschland Erwache 1933" enamel political badge. **$185-$250**

"Heim Ins Reich" political support enamel badge. **$125-$145**

Gild static swastika stickpin. **$65-$85**

NSDAP party affiliate enamel stickpin. **$95-$145**

Nationalsozialitsche Kraftfahrkorps (NSKK)

When Adolf Hitler and the NSDAP waged their political struggle to win over the German people, mobility of their members become paramount to their success. The perceived number of party members was increased dramatically by manipulating the faithful from city to city and rally to rally.

Hitler was seen "everywhere at once" by keeping a rigorous schedule of speaking to as many people at as many locations as he was physically able to do. Through necessity, and because he loved large and powerful autos (though not a driver himself), Hitler always employed the best models and most trusted drivers available in his travels around the country. This hectic mobile pace helped push the NSDAP to the forefront and into eventual leadership of the German political scene.

A motorized section of the SA was organized in 1930, first as the *Nationalsozialisten Automobil-Korps* (NSAK), then renamed the *Nationalsozialitsche Kraftfahrkorps* (NSKK, National Socialist Motor Corps). The skilled members of the NSKK became major competitors in helping the Nazi party achieve its political goals.

Besides transporting SA members from place to place for political meetings and street marches, the NSKK became a subsidiary paramilitary training ground for the clandestine armed forces started by the Weimar government after Germany's defeat in World War I and accelerated under the leadership of Hitler and the Nazi Party. Membership was comprised of mostly mechanically inclined males, 18 to 45 years old and interested in fast and powerful automobiles, motorcycles, and other forms of ground transportation.

Driving skills, knowledge of traffic laws, and map reading were honed in classrooms and during field exercises. Members were not required to have driver's licenses when joining as it was anticipated that they would learn enough through the organization's courses to become proficient drivers. They were taught all facets of vehicle maintenance including engine rebuilding, body restoration, tire repair, and routine upkeep. The vehicular training was combined with structured military drills and Nazi political indoctrination.

Well-planned road trips to massive party rallies or organized sojourns to places of broad interest were exhilarating adventures for many NSKK members in a time when automobile travel was only a communal mode of transportation for the majority of people in the previous 10 years. As the German war machine began to increase to full gear, many NSKK members moved directly into the mechanized ranks of the Wehrmacht, bringing with them the motoring and repair skills they had learned.

The NSKK separated from the SA in 1934, at which time it became an independent branch of the Nazi Party, swelling to over 350,000 members. The organization was divided into nine *Motorobergruppen* (main state groups) with hundreds of *Motorstandarten* (subgroups) formed by geographical areas. Paramilitary ranks were used within the national NSKK, beginning with Mann and continuing through 17 levels of enlisted soldiers and officers, ending with the *Korpsfuhrer* (the State's highest ranking officer, originally Adolf Huhnlein).

NSKK uniforms were either full dress or service wear, depending on the occasion. Full dress uniforms consisted of a brown shirt (copied from the SA blouse) with black collar tabs containing pips, letters, numbers, stripes, and oak leaves to designate the wearer's group and rank. A patch with a silver-thread stylized eagle mounted over a rotated swastika under an NSKK banner was worn on the right upper sleeve, while on the left sleeve a standard NSDAP armband was placed. Single shoulder boards were worn on the right shoulder to designate group, and as a place for the cross strap to be secured. Military and civilian awards earned by the members were worn in their respective places on the shirtfront. Black riding pants, tan tie, black boots, and black leather belt with cross strap holding a rectangular silver-plated buckle (or double claw buckle) with wreath and eagle completed the uniform. Typical headgear was a black overseas cap with the group's color-coded triangle with a silver wire eagle and swastika sewn to the

left front, followed by a series of stripes, pips, and oak leaves along the side to further designate the wearer's rank.

The service uniform consisted of a brown five-button wool tunic worn over a tan shirt with a black tie. Either straight-leg slacks with shoes or riding pants with boots were worn to complete the uniform. Decorations and embellishments remained the same as the dress uniform. The overseas cap, "coffee can" cap (similar to that worn by the SA, but with an NSKK cap badge and colors), or a brown peaked visor cap with metal

emblems of an eagle over a wreath under an NSKK banner were worn.

When on parade or "walking out," members of the NSKK could wear their NSKK daggers. This dagger was similar to the model 1933 SA dagger with many having group markings stamped into the reverse of the cross guards. Unlike the SA model, the NSKK dagger scabbard had a black anodized (form of metal bluing) or later (on RZM models) black-painted finish. The NSKK short hanging strap was made of black rather than brown leather as used on the SA scabbard. In 1936, Korpsfuhrer Huhnlein added the 1936 pattern NSKK dagger. This change affected the scabbard only, which now hung from an elaborate chained hanger of decorated plates and loops.

While in the field or in shop areas, NSKK men often wore overalls and other coarse work attire because of the type of work performed around heavy machinery. When on the road, wool or leather coats were worn for warmth and protection. A unique leather safety helmet was worn, especially while riding motorcycles. It consisted of a dome-shaped black leather body with earflaps, rear neck protector, and chinstraps with roller buckles. A large metal insignia was attached to the front in one of two forms: an earlier nickel-plated short-winged eagle standing on an oak leaf wreath surrounding a static or canted swastika, and a later long-winged aluminum eagle on wreath and swastika below a banner emblazoned with "NSKK" in black paint.

When in civilian clothing, members proudly wore an NSKK membership pin or stickpin to designate their association with the organization. These pins measured 22mm x 21mm and took the form of the NSKK emblem of eagle on round wreath with swastika under an NSKK banner. The reverse was typically marked with either an RZM number or *Ges Gesch* (abbreviation for "*gesetzlich geschutzt*," patent protected).

Members were issued and required to carry an NSKK "pass" (identification book) while on duty. Their photo, personal information (address, birthdate, etc.), and qualifications for vehicular operation and expertise were recorded in the pass.

As with many groups during the Third Reich, the NSKK manufactured and sold a great quantity of day badges (tinnies) to help fund their sponsored events. In addition, they produced a large number of equipment decals, flags, awards, trophies, and other organization-specific items bearing their insignia.

While many young automobile and motorcycle enthusiasts joined the NSKK in the 1930s to pursue their love of motorsports and fast speed, few of them imagined they would help form the nucleus of Adolf Hitler's newly motorized war machine. Their skills and efforts helped the German Wehrmacht attain early victories in Nazi military conquests, only to be later crushed by the overwhelming might of the combined Allied Forces.

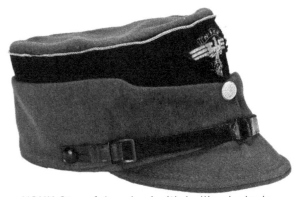

NSKK Sturmfuhrer kepi with bullion insignia. **$1,500-$2,500**

(JAG)

NSKK crash helmet with edelweiss badge. **$795-$1,200**

(JAG)

Silver wire NSKK sleeve eagle. **$65-$85**

NSKK officer's slacks and tunic with armband. **$3,500-$4,900**

(JAG)

Silver wire NSKK overseas cap insignia. **$35-$50**

Gray thread NSKK overseas cap insignia. **$35-$50**

NSKK shoulder board. **$35-$65**

(Private Collection)

NSKK shoulder board. **$35-$45**

(Private Collection)

NSKK 1933 model dagger, maker-marked, with carrying strap. **$650-$950**

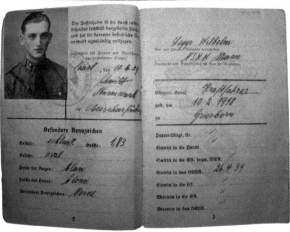

NSKK membership identification booklet. **$145-$225**

NSKK candid photos. **$10-$15**

NSKK metal cap insignia with prongs. **$55-$75**

NSKK cartoon handout for rules of the road. **$45-$50**

NSKK membership pin, RZM-marked. **$65-$85**

Motorsports award stickpin. **$65-$75**

NSKK membership stickpin, RZM-marked. **$65-$85**

Deutscher Luftsportverband (DLV)

Nationalsozialistisches Fliegerkorps (NSFK)

The German people have always been fascinated with all things modern. When practical manned flight became possible, there was no lack of young men and women willing to take up the adventure of flying in the new and somewhat dangerous machines of the day. Many air sports clubs formed across the country to educate enthusiasts and promote the concept of manned flight among the general public through air shows and events. During World War I the German army began using airplanes, at first for enemy observation and aerial recognizance, then later for active combat missions. By the end of the conflict there were an estimated 2,700 airplanes in the Imperial German combat air arsenal.

After Germany's defeat in 1918, the Allied victors wanted to make sure the German nation would no longer be able to wage war on its European neighbors. With the Treaty of Versailles, all German military air wing units and civilian pilots' groups were to be disbanded, and all airplanes and airplane parts, either military or civilian, were to be destroyed or handed over to the Allies. In 1922 the treaty rules were modified to allow a small group of civilian pilots to join other enthusiasts and promote flying. In 1926 the Paris Aviation Agreement modified this again by rescinding all limitations on civilian flyers and aircraft.

When Adolf Hitler and the NSDAP assumed power in 1933, all of the then-existing air sports clubs, along with the flying sections of the SA and the SS, were combined to form the *Deutscher Luftsportverband* (DLV, German Air Sports Organization). The DLV was under the direct control of the Nazi Party, and though seen publicly as a strictly civilian pilot and aircraft organization, was divided into both a civilian group and the *Fliegerschaft* (clandestine air force military training force). Pilots and crewmembers of the future Luftwaffe were trained in the DLV as part of the nation's buildup for the planned European war of expansion.

After application to the DLV, new members (many of whom had been in the Imperial German army air corps) began courses in both aeronautical and basic military training. Membership dues were paid monthly, the receipts of which were recorded with stamps in the individual's DLV ausweis. Training was given in a series of aircraft maintenance programs ranging from engine overhauling to cleaning and patching fabric fuselage sections. Flight instruction generally began with glider flight and progressed into motorized civilian (and later military) aircraft operation.

Because of the Fliegerschaft's clandestine nature, many DLV members wore civilian clothing to hide the group's identity at first, but in time they began to wear smart blue/gray uniforms similar to those worn in the future Luftwaffe. On these tunics, ranking and specialties were acknowledged by the use of colored collar tabs with "gull wing" pips, oak leaves, and silver borders, which were similar to those of the Luftwaffe but differed slightly in hue and size. The peaked blue/gray caps had the distinctive DLV emblem of horizontal silver wings with a vertical propeller cradling a red enamel or painted circle with a rotated black swastika in the center. The back of these devices contained maker's marks and prongs to hold them to the cap fronts. Besides the metal devices, members could purchase more expensive cap devices woven from silver, red, and black bullion thread. This same type of winged insignia was worn by members on civilian clothing in enameled lapel or pinback pins, and could also be seen on standards, vehicle pennants, sports vest emblems, awards, and many other items of the DLV.

As Hitler became bolder and more open in his building of the German military, he decided it was no longer necessary to hide his war machine, and the DLV was dissolved in 1937. At this time, members who did not go directly into the Luftwaffe were transferred to the *Nationalsizialistisches Fliegerkorps* (NSFK), a resurrected flying organization that originally existed from 1931-1932 but had, ironically, been absorbed into the DLV. This organization continued as an air sports club but took on a more martial aspect, training young members with emphasis on instruction for combat flying, tactics,

and military craft maintenance. Model airplane building and competitions for youths as well as snow skiing in the winter months (to enhance pilot coordination) were added to the agenda of new members.

Uniforms changed to paramilitary SA brown shirts (with SA acceptance tags) or steel gray SA-style tunics that replaced the standard DLV uniforms. Collar tabs similar to the SA were used as indicators for rank and specialties. Headwear changed from peaked caps of the DLV to SA-style NSFK "coffee can" caps. The DLV winged swastika design was replaced by the NSFK "Icarus" emblem (Greek mythology's winged man) overlaid with a large swastika on its lower legs.

The cloth emblem with tan background was worn on the right breast pocket of the brown shirt, and with a gray background on the right sleeve of the NSFK tunic. Members were allowed to wear their military and paramilitary awards (such as an iron cross or SA sports badge) on their uniforms when on parade or when walking out. The new NSFK membership pin consisted

of a cross-shaped outstretched Icarus over a half-circle with the letters "NSFK" arched across the top. NSFK sponsors – those nonmembers making monthly support contributions to the group – were given pins consisting of an Icarus above a full circle with the same lettering as the membership pin at the top, but with the addition of the letter "F" at the bottom. These pins came in nickel silver, but changed to a pot metal material as the war progressed and supplies became short.

In addition to membership pins, NSFK men could earn proficiency badges for glider flight, aircraft piloting, or ballooning. A glider badge consisted of a round blue enamel pin, 22mm in diameter, with one to three white "gull wings" across the front, which designated the level of glider proficiency achieved. NSFK flying badges ranged from 45mm to 68mm and followed a general pattern of oval silver wreaths with overlaid balloons, airplanes or gliders, depending on the award bearer's qualification. The back of the awards featured pinback attachments and maker's marks.

Beginning in 1934, DLV officers were permitted to carry daggers with long double-edged blades, winged crossguards, and sun wheel-crested swastika pommels. The rounded handles were covered in dark blue leather with twisted silver wire wraps, while the blue leather-covered scabbard had a silver throat, toe, and linked suspension chains. This sidearm was the predecessor of the first model Luftwaffe dagger, though slightly longer and thinner. Also in 1934, the DLV flyer's knife was introduced – an elegant, short double-edged weapon with blue leather-covered round handle, swept wing crossguard with swastika, rounded pommel cap, and blue leather-covered scabbard. This knife continued to be used by the NSFK after the dissolution of the DLV.

Though the NSFK grew steadily throughout its existence, it never had the volume of members enjoyed by the SA or other paramilitary groups, due in part to its open competition for members with the Luftwaffe. At the 1938 Nuremberg Rally, 73,000 SA men attended the event compared to only 2,400 members of the NSFK.

Although the original air clubs were formed for the positive promotion of flight, the subsequent groups that they became were used by the Nazi regime to build an aggressive force intended for the domination of Europe. Without the DLV and NSFK's early training of young men for aerial combat and support, the Luftwaffe would not have been able to play the major part it did in Hitler's successes and ultimate failures of conquest on the battlefields of Europe.

NSFK service blouse with
SA tag. **$750-$1,000**

DLV chain-stitched insignia
from a flag center. **$75-$125**

NSFK service tunic
with armband.
$950-$1,200

(JAG)

DLV attached set of collar tabs
for a captain. **$125-$150**

22 cal. training rifle with DLV stamped on the receiver. **$850-$1,200**

NSFK gray-backed tunic breast insignia. **$75-$95**

NSFK (marked on scabbard throat) flyer's knife with leather hanger. **$1,200-$1,500**

DLV sports vest insignia. **$65-$85**

DLV vehicle pennant. **$350-$475**

Female glider pilot's ausweis issued by the DLV. **$175-$225**

Glider pilot's license. **$185-$225**

NSFK membership booklet with dues stamps.
$150-$175

Flyer's record book with picture taken in
NSFK service shirt. **$150-$195**

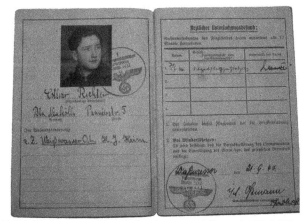

NSFK flight record book for teenaged flyer. **$125-$150**

DLV/HJ comic glider postcard. **$25-$35**

NSFK kepi eagle with prongs. **$135-$150**

DLV plated metal and enamel visor cap badge, maker-marked. **$200-$275**

Glider flight enamel lapel badge. **$125-$150**

Small enamel DLV membership pin. **$75-$85**

Enamel DLV membership lapel pin. **$85-$100**

Large enamel DLV membership pin. **$85-$150**

Flight donation pin. **$75-$85**

1939 NSFK flight event tinnie. **$85-$115**

(Private Collection)

44

DLV event and donation tinnies. **$20-$35**

DLV glider donation tinnie. **$45-$55**

Hermann Goring tinnie for flight support. **$50-$75**

DLV gold metal donation pin. **$50-$65**

DLV plastic event tinnie. **$100-$125**

(Private Collection)

DLV silver metal donation stickpin. **$50-$65**

NSFK supporter membership stickpin. **$75-$95**

1933 day of flight tinnie. **$85-$125**

(Rick Fleury-JAG)

DLV balloonist stickpin. **$450-$575**

Polizei
und
Feuerpolizei

A key promoter of Hitler's ascension to power, and one that he and the members of his immediate circle would later wield without mercy to keep their people under control, was the German police force.

The German police had for many years consisted of an assortment of regional and state forces with little national cohesion. During the Imperial period, control of each group was placed in the hands of local monarchies, and, after the defeat of Germany in World War I, changed to local municipal leadership. The total number of police in the country during the Weimer Republic was to remain under 150,000, have no military training, and be kept distinctly separate from the regular army per the overseeing Allied victors. However, German officials ignored the provisions and slowly grew and trained the police as a clandestine force to augment their limited armed forces.

During the violent periods of the 1920s when street fighting between political factions and public rioting were rampant, many police officials and officers found the emerging Nazi Party, with its charismatic leader, Adolf Hitler, the better choice to support over the equally violent German Communist Party. When called to demonstrations and street brawls, many police helped the Nazis gain the upper hand by arresting their opponents and turning a blind eye to Nazi wrongdoings.

When Hitler came to power, he methodically worked to nationalize and unify the police forces into one centrally controlled unit. The main groups of the new forces were divided into *Schutzpolizei* (uniformed police), *Kriminalpolizei* (criminal police), *Gendarmerie* (rural constables), *Wasserschutzpolizei* (waterway police), *Bahnschutz* (railway police), *Postschutz* (postal police), *Sicherheitspolizei* (security police), and the notorious *Geheime Staatspolizei* (Gestapo, secret state police). These were further divided into smaller subgroups and auxiliaries such as motorized, armored, and mountain police units. When first created, the new national police force reported to Herman Goering as the police minister of Prussia, the largest German state, but by 1936 came under the control of Heinrich Himmler and the *Schutzstaffel* (the SS).

In Germany and later occupied territories, police were assigned to precincts according to population with a range of one officer per 2,000 residents in small villages, to one officer per 600 residents of municipalities up to 100,000 inhabitants. Larger cities were policed by non-municipal state-controlled forces.

In times of emergency, *Hilfpolizei* (police auxiliary) helpers could be called on to assist the regular officers in the duties of crowd control and public protection. One of these groups was the *Landwacht* (national guards), a civilian auxiliary rural police force enlisted to help the Gendarmes. They wore armbands and cap devices that included the word "Landwacht." Women officers served in the plainclothes police units dealing mainly with young female offenders/victims and welfare cases.

The job of the uniformed police was to prevent crimes, protect the citizenry, and later enforce the restrictive wartime Nazi laws in Germany and its occupied territories. As the war progressed, the uniformed police became active combatants assisting the regular armed forces as needed in the field. The criminal police units carried out investigations and detective work. The Gestapo was used primarily to persecute people perceived as internal or external enemies of the regime. Border patrol, waterway safety, traffic control, trainways, postal security, and other police functions were carried out by specialized groups with great efficiency and professionalism.

Enlisted ranking in the Schutzpolizei began with *Anwarter*, followed by *Unterwachtmeister*, *Wachtmeister*, and *Rottwachtmeister*. NCO ranks consisted of *Oberwachtmeister*, *Revieroverwachtmeister*, *Hauptwachtmeister*, *Meister*, *Obermeister*, and *Inspektor*. Officer ranks were *Revier*, *Revierleitnant*, *Revier/Bezirkshauptmann*, *Major*, *Obersleutnant*, *Oberst*, and *General*. After 1942, many top-ranking police generals held both police and SS ranks such as *SS-*

Obergruppenfuhrer und General der Polizei.

In 1936, a standardized set of uniforms replaced the various regional pieces worn by the German police. A well-made Bavarian-style eight silver button, four-pocket light green tunic with dark brown fall-down collars and brown cuffs was introduced for service and parade wear. Light wool or gabardine was used for unlisted ranks, while officers and NCOs could have custom uniforms made of better materials. Collar tabs were either silver or green for urban police or silver on orange for rural constables. Ranking was shown by a

combination of collar tabs, piping and shoulder board variations in braiding, materials and pips. Ranking devices for general officers changed in 1942, from the army style bullion *litzen* (lace) look to the SS-style oak leaf wreath and pip combinations. Shoulder patches with an oval oak leaf wreath overlaid with a spread-winged eagle holding a round wreath surrounding a rotating swastika were worn on the left mid-sleeve. Urban police patches were in green thread with black swastikas, while rural patches were in orange and black. Officers tended to wear silver and black bullion arm patches; general officers wore richly colored gold and black bullion devices. Specialty patches, such as lightning bolts for signal corps, could be worn on the lower left sleeve above the cuff line. Matching trousers or riding pants were worn along with shoes or boots. Belts, cross straps, and other exposed leather accoutrements were usually in black for urban police and brown for rural police. Buckles for enlisted men

were silver rectangles with round oak leaf wreaths surrounding a swastika poised on end.

Officers wore a round version buckle with either a leather or brocade belt. A policeman could wear both his civilian and military decorations in their respective places on his tunic while on duty. Ancillary police units wore varying uniforms such as white tunics and pants with gilded buttons and red insignia for traffic control, or black panzer wrappers with green piping for armored police troops. Long trenchcoats of wool or gabardine were worn over the basic uniform during colder weather. Headgear was comprised of a unique police shako with a rounded green felt-covered body, flat leather-covered top, and front and rear leather visors. A large aluminum broad-winged eagle with swastika over an oak leaf wreath was affixed to the shako front. Officers wore a bullion national oval cockade and silver fishscale chinstrap (gold for general officers), while the enlisted cockade was tri-color aluminum with a leather chinstrap. Horsehair plumes were added to the front above the faceplates and behind the cockades during parades. Shakos were worn until the advent of war, after which they were replaced with more utilitarian headgear. Visor caps with green bodies, brown bands, and green or orange piping were commonly worn, as were green overseas caps. Each had front insignia of aluminum or silver with police eagle, wreath, and swastika combinations. M-43 visor caps were used later in the war as were light steel (and sometimes heavy combat as duty dictated) helmets painted black or green with police and national decals on the sides. If assigned to a motorcycle unit, officers wore a leather (black, brown, or white) protective crash helmet with aluminum police emblem affixed to the front.

Police often wore a long stag-handled bayonet with the police emblem attached to the outward handle. The nickel-plated crossguard contained oak leaf engraving, and the pommel had a slotted or unslotted eagle head design. These impressive bayonets were housed in either black or brown leather scabbards (depending on branch of service) and were often unit-marked on the crossguard reverse.

Swords were worn during parade and dress occasions. These consisted of a slender plated or polished blade with a distinctive thin-handled "D" guard. The handle was of black composite surrounded by an evenly spaced coil of silver wire. A silver or silver-plated police emblem was inlaid on the outer grip. Enlisted swords had a smooth, rounded pommel cap; officer swords had a double-fluted round pommel. Each sword was carried in a black-painted steel scabbard with ornately carved silver drags and throats.

At the outbreak of war, police typically carried sidearms or rifles while on duty. Pistols were sheltered in black or brown flap holsters, and ammunition pouches hung from belts for those carrying rifles or machine pistols. When involved in combat or anti-partisan operations, police units were issued any and all of the normal weapons available to regular army troops.

Full-time police officers were expected to carry identification in the form of a *Dienstausweis* (service identity document). The green oilcloth booklet bore the owner's photo with overstamps, information as to name, rank and assignments, and what firearms he was authorized to carry. Members of the criminal and state security police units carried *Dienstmarken* (warrant discs): oval-shaped metal disks with police emblems and individual serial numbers. These identification disks often allowed unlimited, unquestioned access and searches of property by the bearer.

Firefighting groups had existed to protect the citizens and property in Germany for hundreds of years, especially around areas of high population, or, after the Industrial Revolution, in areas of dense manufacturing. With total control and centralization of power in mind, Hitler's government mandated that local fire departments become part of a national agency, the *Feuerschutzpolizei* (fire protection police) in 1938. As part of the regular police force, fire departments now came under the command of the national police force. The fire police were broken down into *Zugwache* (watch squad, the smallest unit) and the larger *Gruppenwache* (watch group). The number of firefighting units was determined on an individual basis with the general population and likelihood of fires occurring (industries, plants, etc.) taken into consideration. The maximum age for a professional firefighter was 60 years. All officers were trained at the Fire Protection Officers School at Eberswalde. In larger cities with populations over 150,000, the *Freiwillige Feuerwehren* (volunteer

fire defense service) was organized to complement the full-time units. In cases where full-time and volunteer units could not handle the work, such as following massive Allied airstrikes during the war, then *Pflichtfeuerwehr* (obligatory fire service) units were created to help.

Full-time and volunteer firefighters wore dark blue uniforms with carmine red piping, matching piped trousers, black leather belts with silver buckles, black leather shoes, and either a peaked overseas cap or a unique fireman's helmet. The tunics followed the police style with red-backed collar tabs and shoulder boards. A fireman's insignia consisted of a carmine-colored eagle with outstretched wings clutching an oak leaf circle surrounding a swastika. This was mounted on an oval oak leaf wreath and bore the name of the *Bezirk* (district) above the wreath. Officer's insignia were made of bullion thread and did not have the district name included on the top. Insignias were worn on the left sleeves of the tunics. A fireman's service belt was a double-wide leather belt with a unique oval loop attachment on the front designed for hooking onto a rope while carrying out firefighting functions. Beautiful peaked caps of dark blue had black mohair bands, carmine piping, and silver police metal insignia of an eagle, swastika, and wreath, over which was mounted a cockade bearing the national colors. Enlisted peaked caps bore black leather chinstraps; officers' chinstraps were made of silver wire flecked with carmine accents. The overseas cap was of dark blue material with a cloth (for enlisted) or bullion (for officers) police device sewn to the front edge. The fire police helmet was a black thin-gauged steel shell with police and national decals on the sides, a nickel silver or aluminum comb (many were produced with or without these), and detachable leather neckguard and chinstrap.

As the war progressed and centralization of power became more pronounced, fire police uniforms began to change to a green color with black cuffs and carmine piping. However, the dark blue uniforms continued to be worn until the end of the war. In 1942 a series of silver embroidered proficiency cloth badges were introduced for volunteer firefighters; these badges consisted of small steering wheel insignias for drivers and oak leaves with pips for different levels of district leaders.

When on parade or walking out, many enlisted and non-commissioned officer firemen wore dress bayonets. Fire police dress bayonets have a basic design of polished or plated single-edged blade with black plastic riveted grips, nickel-plated bird's-head pommel, and S-shaped nickel crossguard. These could be embellished with sawback or engraved blades and were carried in black leather frogs with carmine and silver portepeeds. NCO bayonets were of the same design as those worn by enlisted men but had shorter blades with clipped points (false top edges).

Officers' daggers were first designed in the 1870s and were worn throughout the Third Reich period. The long, etched double-edged dagger had a black leather-wrapped handle, nickel-plated spiral pommel, and stylized crossguard with helmet and ax relief designs. Officers also carried swords with simple nickel-plated "D" guards, etched blades, and black wire-wrapped handles. The scabbards were black leather with silver-mounted fittings.

Service axes were worn during parades, and rare presentation axes were awarded for long or meritorious service. These could be elaborately engraved works of art with beautiful wooden handles and commemorative shields.

Police fire helmet with comb and neck protector.
$575-$800

(JAG)

Police light helmet.
$450-$700

Two decorations were created to honor firefighters: the *Feuerwehr Ehrenzeichen* (Fire Brigade Decoration) 1st and 2nd classes were introduced in 1936. The 2nd class was a round silver ring with the words "Fur Verdienste im Feuerloschwesen" ("For Merit in the Fire Brigade Organization") over which was mounted a 43mm white enamel cross bearing a red flame on each arm supporting a canted swastika encircled in the center. This was suspended by a ball loop from a white and red ribbon and awarded for 25 years of service as a firefighter. The 1st class award was in the same configuration as the 2nd class award but was produced as a pinback version without a suspension ring or ribbon. In 1938, the 1st class pinback was eliminated and reintroduced in the suspended 2nd class form in a gilded rather than silver finish.

As the Nazi regime engulfed more territories and the police forces became more intertwined with the SS, some uniformed and plainclothes police formations, especially those in the eastern occupied areas, became responsible for carrying out of Himmler's brutal policies toward the conquered peoples. What had once been members of a well-disciplined, respectable and efficient system became participants in immoral actions that Nazi propaganda led them to perform without question.

Forced labor, ethnic cleansing, and other atrocities were carried out by some units with little or no concern for the welfare of the general public. At the end of the war many instigators discarded their identifications and melted into the droves of displaced peoples. Though small in number compared to the majority of police who did their civil service honorably, the behavior of these participants have left a stigma on the German police forces that will last for generations to come.

When Allied incendiary bombing raids created devastating firestorms across Germany, the fire police faced insurmountable deeds on a daily basis. Lack of equipment, water cutoffs, and the danger associated with the sheer magnitude of increasing fires often proved too much for the firemen to handle. Thousands of these brave souls perished while trying to save their cities from the ultimate destruction of a worthless cause.

With the defeat of Adolf Hitler and the Nazis, the Allied victors enlisted the German police and fire police to keep order in the devastation that remained of Germany. Because of their ability to assist in the rebuilding of social order, police formations helped play a major part in creating one of the leading democracies in today's Europe.

M43 cap for armored police vehicle crewmember. **$1,000-$1,250**

Border guard visor cap. **$650-$800**

Urban police enlisted shako. **$750-$950**

Fire police officer's visor cap. **$675-$850**

Urban police enlisted officer's visor cap, dated 1942. **$700-$850**

Rural police enlisted shako. **$850-$1,150**

Dusseldorf urban Wachtmeister police tunic with sports badges and party pin. **$1,100-$1,350**

Rural police field tunic converted from an Austrian service shirt. **$450-$650**

Rural constable's Innsbruck tunic with SA badge. **$900-$1,100**

Army field police tunic. **$850-$1,100**

Police general officer collar tabs. **$1,300-$1,500**

Police general officer shoulder boards. **$950-$1,100**

Police officer bullion sleeve eagle. **$135-$175**

Police general officer bullion sleeve eagle and wreath. **$950-$1,200**

Rural police constable sleeve eagle. **$75-$85**

Rural police trenchcoat. **$550-$700**

Urban police officer's trousers. **$450-$500**

Sleeve patch attributed to the 1936 Olympic village police force. **$450-$600**

Fire police officer bullion overseas cap eagle. **$75-$85**

Large police sports vest eagle and wreath. **$95-$125**

Fire police sleeve eagles and wreaths with district names. **$55-$75**

Fire police sports vest eagle and wreath. **$75-$95**

Border guard cloth cap emblem set. **$45-$55**

Small police sports vest eagle and wreath. **$75-$85**

Border guard cuff title. **$145-$175**

Landwacht auxiliary police duty armband. **$145-$175**

Border guard shoulder board. **$45-$65**

Prison official's shoulder board. **$65-$95**

(Private Collection)

Unissued banded urban police shoulder boards. **$65-$85**

Unissued banded rural police shoulder boards with Austrian maker paper tag. **$95-$125**

Fire police NCO shoulder boards. **$45-$55**

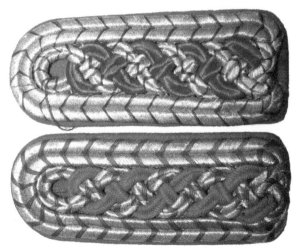

Fire police officer's shoulder boards. **$55-$75**

Border guard bullion collar tab. **$45-$65**

Three-place ribbon bar with 2nd Class iron cross, war merit service cross, and police long service award. **$95-$135**

WHW plastic autobahn police officer. **$35-$45**

Army field police duty gorget. **$675-$850**

Police whistle with an SS eagle attached to a tri-color woven cord. **$650-$800**

Police enlisted officer's belt buckle. **$145-$175**

Fire police NCO short clip point dress bayonet. **$225-$325**

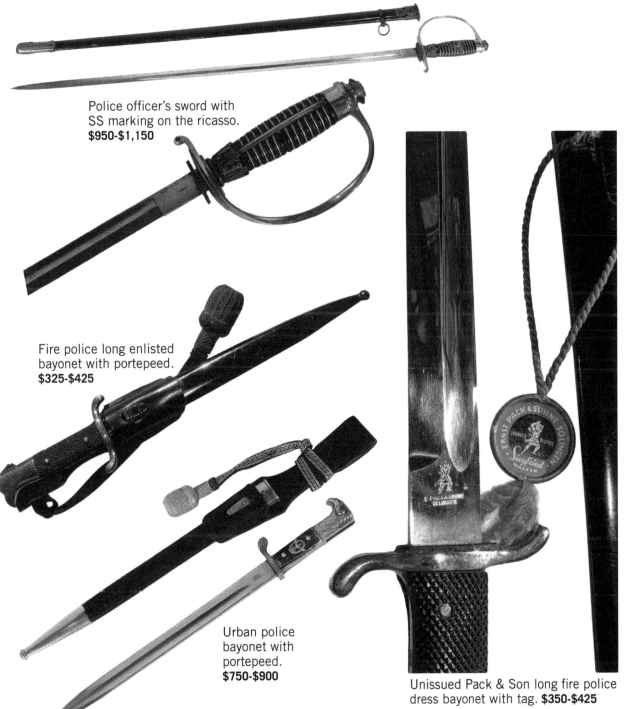

Police officer's sword with portepeed. **$900-$1,100**

Police officer's sword with SS marking on the ricasso. **$950-$1,150**

Fire police long enlisted bayonet with portepeed. **$325-$425**

Urban police bayonet with portepeed. **$750-$900**

Unissued Pack & Son long fire police dress bayonet with tag. **$350-$425**

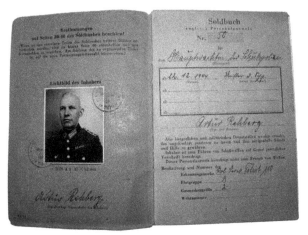

Police NCO soldbuch. **$175-$250**

Border guard service ausweis. **$150-$185**

Rural police death memorial card. **$35-$45**

1941 police pocket calendar and fact booklet. **$125-$150**

Fire police officer ausweis. **$85-$125**

Metal shako plate with attaching prongs. **$125-$150**

Fire police visor cap eagle and wreath. **$75-$95**

Police officer visor cap eagle and wreath. **$75-$95**

Border guard gilded sleeve shield. **$150-$175**

1942 police tinnie. **$45-$55**

Landwacht police auxiliary cap eagle and wreath. **$125-$145**

Police general officer or autobahn officer visor eagle and cockade. **$145-$165**

Fire police 1st class service award, maker-marked. **$350-$500**

1934 desktop souvenir for police rally. **$475-$600**

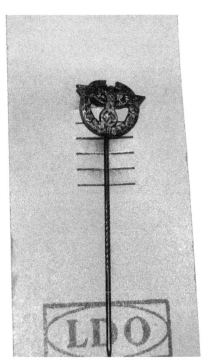

Police membership stickpin on original LDO company card. **$125-$150**

6

Reichs Arbeitsdienst (RAD)

Beginning after World War I, a national mandatory labor service had been proposed by many administrators within the German government. Like the Civilian Conservation Corps of the 1930s in the United States, the original intent of this movement was to provide work for the unemployed and improve the infrastructure of the country by building and repairing roads, bridges, and public buildings.

In the late 1920s the *Stahlhelm* (Steel Helmet, the largest German veterans league and paramilitary group) started regional voluntary labor groups called *Freiwillige Arbeitsdienst* (FAD, volunteer labor service). These groups employed many out-of-work individuals during the rabid unemployment of the Great Depression and served as a clandestine military training ground to circumvent the Allies' restrictions placed on the German military.

When Adolf Hitler came to power, the labor corps was seen as the perfect way to enhance the military training of German youth, continue to increase employment, and foster the political indoctrination of the workers. Constantine Hierl, a decorated army staff officer and early Hitler advocate, was chosen as the labor corps leader under the new regime.

As with many organizations within the Nazi dictatorship, the regional labor corps was consolidated for centralized control into a national corps and renamed the *Reichs Arbeitsdeinst* (RAD, National Labor Corps). The corps was divided into *Inspectorate, Arbeitsgaue, Gruppen, Abteilungen, Zuge,* and *Truppe.* Each Truppe consisted of 15 *Arbeitsmunner* commanded by a *Truppfuhrer* and *Vormann.* Structured military training became the main emphasis of the new organization, along with organizing labor for the reclamation of farmland to feed the growing population and having men of all social status working side-by-side to develop the Nazi principle of eliminating class distinctions by promoting a common *Volk* (people).

The RAD's membership increased significantly in 1934 when it changed from a strictly voluntary institution to one with male conscription of a six-month tour of duty. In 1935 a national law made service in the RAD mandatory for both young males and females, causing even greater growth for the organization; 54,000 RAD members marched in the 1935 Nuremberg Rally. However, the RAD eventually found itself competing for members with the military forces and civilian manufacturing in the late 1930s.

As the German war machine began to ramp up for the forthcoming conflicts, the *wehrmacht* inducted new recruits before they went into the RAD labor service. Likewise, the war materials industry called for more workers to equip the new German military forces. Through the leadership of Hierl, the RAD remained intact through these trying times and, as the war began, was assigned to assist the armed services in the building of roads, bridges, barracks, and airfields, and with general repairs. When the war dragged on and began to decimate the ranks of the military, the RAD members attached to these units began to assume a more active role in combat operations. By the end of the war, RAD groups were considered full-fledged military units and took part in the final battles on the Eastern Front and in the streets of Berlin.

The uniforms of the early FAD members consisted of plain brown work shirts with insignia, matching pants or britches, a billed cap with emblem, and later, an NSDAP armband. FAD emblems took the form of an upturned square-topped spade with wheat stalks branching out on either side. After the Nazi party came to power, the RAD insignia gradually took the place of the FAD. Emblems were similar, but the spade changed to a round-topped shovel, the wheat stalks were redesigned, and a prominent swastika was positioned over the front of the shovel blade. Both FAD and RAD insignia was placed on uniforms, sports vest patches, cap badges, buckle plates, flagpole finials, and metal membership pins.

RAD members wore a six-button earth brown wool tunic with a dark brown collar. If open-collared, it was worn with a brown shirt, black tie, brown pants or britches, black belt with rectangular buckle, boots or shoes, and either an earth brown overseas cap or a billed "Alpine-style" cap unique to the RAD.

The leader's and enlisted men's tunics were similar in cut and color (though the leaders could have better-quality materials used in custom-made pieces) as the philosophy stressed the non-recognition of class. A distinctive *Dienststellenabzeichen* (assignment shield) was worn on the left upper arm of the RAD tunic and featured a series of letters and numbers that designated the wearer's assignment, such as battalion, section, and group. Beginning in November 1943, the shields were left blank and a rectangular cloth header was added, showing the unit information. Various colors of white, red, and gold were used to further show rank and position. Ranks and specialties were also shown through collar patches and shoulder boards. Belts with or without cross straps were of black leather or brocade for leader's dress, with rectangular buckles bearing the RAD emblem of shovel, wheat and swastika. Open claw buckles were also worn. Leaders sported a round buckle with the RAD emblem. Both military and civilian awards could be worn on the tunic fronts in their respective positions.

On dress occasions or when walking out, an enlisted man or leader could wear a dagger. The 40cm, 19-ounce *Haumesser* (hewer) was a combination of both dress and utility, having a massive, slightly curved blade and stag handles. Hewers were first used by all ranks from 1934 to 1937, after which time a new model leader's dagger was introduced. At nine ounces and 39cm, this lighter and smaller 1937 weapon featured a distinct eagle-headed pommel, white plastic or ivory grips, and a lighter arched blade. The blade inscription on both models was *Arbeit Adelt* (Work Ennobles).

Overseas caps worn by members bore the RAD emblem on the front, in colored cotton for enlisted men or finer bullion thread for leaders. The unique *Tuchmutze* (cloth billed cap), designed by Hierl, consisted of an earth brown body with folded side flaps, matching soft bill, and wide, dark brown cap band with RAD insignia in metal, cloth or bullion affixed to the front. Traditions badges were authorized for some of the groups to wear on the sides of their caps, designating pride in their regions or an historical event. When in civilian clothing, members could wear the RAD membership pinback or stickpins on their coat lapels to show their affiliation.

Women played a major role in the RAD, having their own sections (RADwj, Labor Service of Female Youth), which helped with childrearing, food production, and clerical work. The more loosely controlled national organization was divided into 29 *Bezirke* (districts).

The female dress tunic consisted of earth brown material with dark brown collar, brown skirt, white blouse, and brown/green fedora hat bearing the district RADwj emblem of a cutout oval encircling a canted swastika and wheat stalks. Their district patch was worn on their left sleeve, and rank was shown by wearing collar tresses, shield colors, and a series of badges worn at the top closure of their blouses. These round badges were 44mm and carried a canted swastika above wheat shafts in the center. The first series had "Sutterlin script" writing around the outside edge: *"Arbeit fur dein Volk. Adelt dich Selbst. Deutscher Frauenarbeitsdeinst"* (Work for your people. Ennoble yourself. German Women's Labor Service). Later models bore plain, ringed, or woven-edge borders. Badges came in iron, silver, or gold coloring to further designate rank and position. If a woman was a Nazi party member, she could wear her enamel membership badge on the left lapel of the tunic.

Both male and female members of the RAD were required to carry identification books that held a photo, personal information about the carrier, and their current RAD assignment. Awards of the RAD were sparse, though career members were recognized with long service awards that consisted of an oval medal with oak leaf border surrounding the RAD emblem of shovel and wheat stalks. The reverse was inscribed, *"Fur treue Dienste im Reicharbeitsdienst"* (For loyal service in the national labor service). The awards were suspended from cornflower blue ribbons and were bestowed for four, 12, 18, and 25 years of service, differentiated by bronze, silver, and gilded surfaces. RAD members made mandatory contributions to the "Arbeits Dank" organization, a body charged with caring for those injured during their RAD service, helping indigent members, and providing insurance.

As the conflict continued and thousands of army, navy, and air force personnel were killed or wounded, RAD members became increasingly involved with antiaircraft gunnery, manning fortifications, and actual field combat in addition to their duties of rebuilding the wreckage left by the war. Though they lacked the specialized training that many of their counterparts in the regular military had received, the RAD members fought and died valiantly, driven by the influence of propaganda promoting what they believed were just causes in the Third Reich.

Unissued and unassigned RAD male sleeve patch. **$45-$50**

RAD enlisted man's wool overcoat with armband. **$575-$750**

RAD tunic with armband. **$950-$1,250**

(JAG)

RAD cloth cap badge. **$40-$50**

RAD male sports vest cloth emblem. **$45-$65**

Unissued late war RAD male sleeve patch. **$45-$50**

Female RAD high leader sleeve shield. **$795-$850**

(Private Collection)

RAD female sports vest patch. **$55-$75**

(Private Collection)

Leader grade female RAD sleeve patch with unit markings. **$75-$85**

RAD enlisted shoulder boards. **$45-$65**

RAD enlisted buckle with leather fob. **$145-$175**

Four-piece RAD women's grouping with identifications and membership throat broach. **$350-$450**

RAD enlisted belt and buckle. **$165-$225**

GI factory-recovered RAD buckle strikes. **$175-$225**

Twelve-piece paper grouping for young RAD women, including other identifications and paperwork. **$375-$450**

FAD enlisted belt buckle. **$95-$125**

FAD ausweis. **$95-$125**

Arbeits Dank membership identification. **$55-$75**

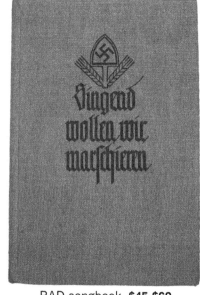

RAD songbook. **$45-$60**

RAD female ausweis. **$95-$125**

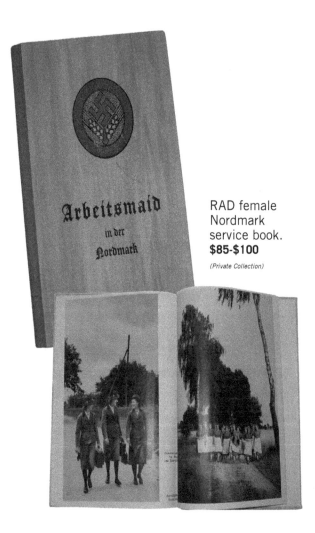

RAD female Nordmark service book. **$85-$100**

(Private Collection)

Female RAD
photos. **$15-$20**

(Private Collection)

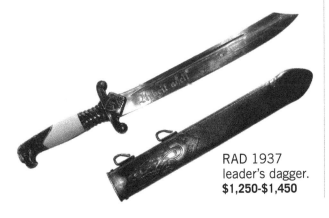

Female RAD camp flag, 4 ft. x 8 ft. **$425-$525**

RAD hewer with
scabbard. **$750-$950**

RAD high leader cufflinks. **$850-$950**

Arbeits Dank
membership
ring in silver and
enamel. **$350-$425**

RAD 1937
leader's dagger.
$1,250-$1,450

RAD four-year-long
service medal with
ribbon. **$175-$225**

RAD 12-year-long
service medal with
ribbon. **$225-$275**

RAD painted metal cap badge with prongs. **$55-$65**

FAD cap badge with prongs. **$45-$65**

RADwj war helper's badge. **$95-$135**

Bronze RAD female fedora badge. **$125-$135**

Silver RAD female fedora badge. **$95-$125**

(Private Collection)

Late-war zinc RAD fedora badge. **$55-$65**

RAD female high leader commemorative badge. **$950-$1,100**

(Private Collection)

First design Frauenarbeitsdienst badge in gold, serial numbered on reverse. **$285-$350**

(Private Collection)

Early bronze female 1937 Frauenarbeitsdienst badge, serial numbered on reverse. **$225-$275**

Silver Frauenarbeitsdienst badge, first design until 1937, serial numbered on reverse. **$225-$275**

RAD female gold mid-level Stabsoberfuhrerin neck badge. **$275-$300**

(Private Collection)

Silver high level Maidenhauptfuhrerin female neck badge. **$225-$275**

(Private Collection)

RAD female silver mid-level Maidenoberfuhrerin neck badge. **$250-$285**

(Private Collection)

RAD female bronze mid-level Maidenunterfuhrerin neck badge. **$225-$250**

Gold high level Stabshauptfuhrerin female neck badge. **$285-$325**

Bronze high level Maidenfuhrerin female neck badge. **$235-$275**

(Private Collection)

Arbeits Dank membership enamel badge. **$55-$75**

Arbeits Dank honor enamel badge. $150-$175

Braunschweig state labor service badge. $175-$200

Male RAD membership enamel pin. $65-$75

FAD membership enamel pin. $95-$125

Bronze RADwj commemorative brooch for completed service. $125-$150

Silver RADwj commemorative brooch for completed service. $125-$150

RAD RADwj old silver neck brooch with variant oversized pin. $175-$250

(Private Collection)

RAD RADwj old silver neck broach for lower ranks. $125-$165

RAD female neck brooch in bronze for Jungfuhrerin. $95-$125

RAD female neck brooch in iron for Arbeitsmaid. $95-$125

RAD female neck brooch in gold for Stabsfuhrerin. $125-$175

1934 RAD Gau tinnie. $125-$165

Gold FAD membership stickpin. $50-$60

Silver FAD membership stickpin. $45-$55

Male RAD membership enamel badge on stickpin. $65-$85

Deutsches
Arbeitsfront
(DAF)

With the domination of Europe and the Russian East as their main goals, the armed forces of Hitler's Germany relied heavily on their nation's manufacturing and agricultural concerns to provide them with the arms and supplies they needed. Centralized control of the workforce was imperative to the success of this massive undertaking: As the number of available workers and facilities gradually decreased, military needs exponentially increased.

Hitler understood the importance of an effective labor force and appointed Dr. Robert Ley leader of the newly formed *Deutsches ArbeitFront* (DAF, German Workers' Front) in 1933. With Ley at its head, the DAF immediately gained control of all workers in the German Reich, and in conjunction with the Nazi party was able to direct efforts to meet the State's needs for military buildup.

German unions for technical trades and professional workers had been in existence for hundreds of years throughout Germany. When the DAF was formed after Hitler's assumption to power in 1933, all unions were forcibly incorporated into the DAF. Workers either joined the DAF directly (at first on a voluntary basis, but by 1935 dues were automatically deducted from their wages), or their professional organization became a corporate member or subgroup of the DAF. These professional groups included:

The *Reichsnahrstand* (national providers), started in 1933 as an organization of farmers, farm workers, and agricultural distributors for food production and price controls. Its motto was *Blut und Boden* (blood and soil), and its emblem was a swastika overlaid with a wheat sheaf and sword, sometimes under a folded-wing eagle.

Reichsbund Der Deutschen Beamten, RDB (National Association of German Civil Servants), started in 1933 as a professional group for public officials. Its symbol was a short, straight-winged eagle perched on a canted swastika with "RDB" on its breast.

Deutsche Stenografenschaft (German stenographers guild), started in 1875 as an organization for shorthand and typing professionals. Its emblem was a pen with outstretched wings intertwined with a swastika on its upper shaft.

Reichsverband Deutscher Kleintierzuchter, RDKL (association for small animal breeders), started in 1933 as an organization for the promotion of breeding rabbits, honeybees, and other small domestic animals. Its emblem was a closed-wing eagle with swastika on its breast, resting on a bar with the letters "RDKL."

Nationalsozialistische Betriebszellenorganisation, NSBO (NS factory labor group), started in 1928 as an organization of factory technicians promoting unionism and the Nazi cause. Its emblem was a hand holding a staff with a swastika on top, attached to a gear with the letters "NSBO" across the face.

Naitionalsozialistischer Rechtswahrerbund, NSRB (NS legal professional association), started in 1928 as an organization of attorneys, judges, and other legal workers. Its emblem was an eagle with a rotated swastika on its chest, standing on an upturned sword holding balanced scales.

Nationalsozialistische Lehrerbund, NSLB (NS teachers association), started in 1929 as the national organization for teachers to promote their craft. Its emblem was an eagle perched on a swastika with the letters "NSLB" above.

Pay levels were strictly controlled by the government, so other inducements were used to increase active participation in the DAF. Members joined in order to gain promotion within their companies or industries, to compete in the series of well-regulated competitions continually being staged, and to take advantage of *Kraft durch Freude Betreung* (strength through joy – welfare). The KDF organization provided inexpensive vacation trips and other leisure activities for workers who would have not been able to afford them. DAF recruitment of new members was so successful that membership increased from five million members in 1933 to over 25 million members in 1942.

With Robert Ley's administration firmly in control, the Nazi party was able to direct all education and skilled and unskilled trade activity as well as produce goods and services deemed fit for the continuation of the war. Prices of all goods were fixed by the Nazi State, and despite the increased use of resources for military production as the war progressed, Hitler insisted that consumer goods still be produced in abundance to give the impression to the average German that life was continuing as normal.

Members in DAF subgroups, such as the teacher or civil servant organizations, did not typically wear uniforms but relied on their membership pins to show their involvement in a particular organization. Rank and file DAF members wore their membership pins on a daily basis. The pin consisted of a nickel silver, aluminum, or white metal gear with a static or rotated swastika in the center, in either stickpin or pinback design. Variations had a solid or cut-out center backing, and most were manufacturer code (RZM)-marked on the reverse.

For parades, festivals, and special meetings, regular members of the DAF wore *Festzanzug der DAF* (festive uniforms) consisting of a civilian-style double-breasted dark blue suit with matching pants, vest, white shirt, black tie, and black dress shoes. The black plastic buttons on the jacket bore facsimiles of the DAF membership pin. The jacket lining was white

with alternating lines and "DAF" printed throughout. Members wore DAF membership pins on the lapel along with any military/paramilitary awards they had earned, and a standard NSDAP armband on the left sleeve. A dark blue peaked cap with oak leaf band, black leather or composite visor, gilded oval swastika, and oak leaf badge topped off the festive uniform.

In 1934 Dr. Ley created *Werkscharen* (work squads – political shock troops) to help control membership and promote the Nazi philosophy among workers. To strengthen this ideal, in 1939 Ley ordered all Werkscharen leaders to become NSDAP political leaders. Hitler allowed Ley to develop this small private labor army but kept it unarmed and relatively small in numbers.

Uniforms worn by Werkscharen members consisted of a waist-length dark blue wool jacket and matching riding pants, tan shirt, black tie, and full black boots. Rank was designated through piped shoulder straps, DAF pips, and rank chevrons. An over-the-shoulder cross strap was sometimes attached to the belt with a rectangular cogwheel and swastika DAF buckle. A standard NSDAP armband was worn on the left sleeve along with a membership pin and military/paramilitary awards on the left breast. A dark blue overseas cap with a national eagle and swastika completed the official uniform, though unofficially a DAF pin was used instead on the cap front. In addition, a dark blue visor cap was introduced in 1938 with silver or gilded insignia, depending on rank, of an elongated wreath with cogwheel-enclosed swastika under an eagle perched on a smaller round wreath and swastika.

The DAF swastika and cogwheel were used liberally on many DAF festival day badges sold to support events. It was also used on DAF party flags, documents, and sports vest patches. A striking diamond-shaped black cloth-backed aluminum DAF device was sewn onto many other paramilitary uniforms to designate the wearer's dual membership with the DAF organization. Large aluminum DAF wall plaques were sold to merchants and businessmen to be hung in their businesses to show support for the organization. Standard flags featured the DAF symbol in the center with district patches sewn on the upper corner.

DAF sporting events were promoted to build camaraderie, pitting groups of workers from different companies against each other in a variety of sports. Competitions were also held in overall manufacturing production and in excellence of craftsmanship. Winners not only had the prestige of winning, but were often awarded prizes such as KDF trips abroad. KDF programs made events such as vacation trips and opera and theater visits affordable to average workers – things most of them could not have attained before the Nazis came to power. Ocean cruises on liners such as the Wilhelm Gustaf became possible with the help of KDF programs. The Volkswagen (people's car, originally called the KDF Wagon) was a KDF project started so that all workers could own an automobile on an affordable payment plan.

KDF insignia consisted of a pinwheel-design circle with a rotated swastika in the center. This design can be found on many of the event badges, membership pins, group flags, and armbands worn by KDF workers.

Frauenamt der DAF (women's groups of the DAF) were also organized. Members were indoctrinated with the Nazi system of belief and worked to improve workplace issues, though equality of pay was never achieved. In 1937 a series of triangular badges was produced consisting of a black enamel background with a silver DAF cogwheel swastika in the center. Level of leadership was shown on the badges by the addition of different borders of colored enamel or oak leaf trim.

As a part of the NSDAP under the control of the DAF, the *NS Frauenschaft* (Nazi women's group) offered *Deutscher Frauenhilfdienst* (German women's help service) to female DAF members – childcare

or shopping assistance when work prevented DAF members from completing normal domestic duties. Help with work at home and a chance for equality with men in the workplace, along with other benefits of the DAF, lured many women into the Frauenamt ranks.

As another controlling factor of the DAF, the organization was appointed the *Treu hander* (trustee) for all foreign workers employed in the Reich. They fed and housed workers in barracks on or near the work grounds. Foreign workers wore identifying patches such as the *Ostabzeichen* (East badge) consisting of a white "Ost" on a blue background. These workers supplemented the German workforce and were vital to wartime production.

While the war progressed, German industry was called upon again and again to produce the necessary materials to feed the fighting power of the German armed forces. As factories were bombed and supplies cut off, workers found themselves in increasingly more dangerous locations. Through the enforcement of constant propaganda and political indoctrination, workers continued to produce at astounding rates until the end of the regime and its surrender to the Allied Forces.

DAF festive visor cap. **$275-$325**

DAF overseas cap. **$250-$325**

DAF sleeve insignia, RZM tag on reverse. **$125-$150**

DAF festive suit with double-breasted coat, vest and pants, armband, medal bar, party pin, and tinnie. **$1,150-$1,350**

DAF festive cap badge with prongs. **$45-$65**

DAF woven cap eagle and wreath. **$65-$85**

DAF buckle with leather fob. **$150-$175**

DAF sports vest patch. **$75-$85**

Foreigner workbook, work record book for a Polish girl. **$75-$95**

NSBO (labor cell) group sports vest patch. **$75-$90**

Foreigner workbook and Eastern workers patch, which is worn in the book photo. **$125-$150**

DAF sports annual record book. **$125-$150**

Standard early issue workbook of employment history. **$25-$40**

DAF membership and dues book. **$45-$55**

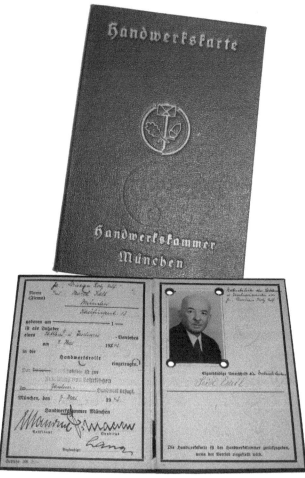

Craft guild membership book. **$95-$125**

Business association membership ausweis and cover. **$75-$95**

DAF members with festive caps. **$5-$10**

"Strength through joy" membership folk dance event bi-fold card. **$35-$45**

Stenographers guild membership ausweis for a young girl. **$145-$165**

DAF desk ornament, chrome on steel. **$150-$175**

DAF wall plaque. **$225-$275**

DAF unit flagpole shield. **$250-$300**

"Strength through joy" trip souvenir bracelet. **$275-$325**

DAF Ortsgruppe standard, 4 ft. **x 4 ft. $450-$575**

DAF furniture or equipment tag. **$35-$45**

Farmers organization flag and enamel long service pin. **$250-$375**

Stenographers guild two-sided hand-sewn table banner with city emblem on reverse. **$625-$750**

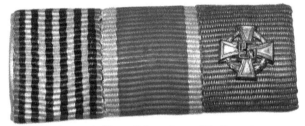

Three-place civilian ribbon bar with Prussian war effort cross, social welfare, and civic long service awards. **$45-$65**

Bavarian industrial service medal and issue box. **$375-$450**

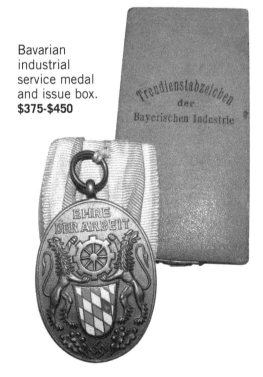

Lapel pin for the Bavarian industry merit medal. **$25-$45**

Standard 25-year civil long service award with case. **$150-$175**

Standard 40-year civil long service award with case. **$225-$250**

First model variant 50-year civil long service award with ribbon. **$250-$375**

Bavarian industry merit medal. **$150-$250**

DAF skiing competition event badge, 1938-1939. **$95-$125**

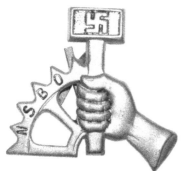

NSBO metal cap badge with prongs. **$75-$85**

Small animal breeders association honor pin. **$150-$175**

1933 meeting badge for the German teachers league. **$225-$250**

(Private Collection)

Folk art promotional badge, enamel, maker-marked. **$60-$75**

Berlin dentist organization meeting pin, enamel. **$75-$95**

DAF women's Frauenamt membership pin, Gau level. **$250-$300**

DAF women's Frauenamt membership pin, entry level. **$150-$175**

Construction trade enamel membership pin. **$65-$85**

DAF aluminum membership pin, RZM-marked. **$35-$45**

NSAO, NS association for work victims membership pin. **$65-$85**

GAO, work victims association membership pin. **$65-$85**

DAOV, work victims welfare membership pin. **$65-$85**

Stenographers guild enamel membership pin. **$75-$100**

Nazi teachers association membership pin, type 2, enamel. **$125-$175**

Small animal breeders association membership pin. **$45-$65**

Government workers association membership pin. **$55-$75**

Craftsmen's guild membership lapel pin. **$65-$85**

1935 day of work event tinnie, maker-marked on reverse, pinback. **$25-$35**

Aircraft industry merit award, enamel pinback. **$185-$250**

DAF membership pin, cutout with rotated swastika, RZM-marked. **$45-$65**

DAF solid-back alloy membership stickpin, RZM-marked. **$35-$45**

Farmers and food producers organization long service award in bronze, pinback. **$150-$185**

Farmers and food producers organization long service award in silver, pinback. **$175-$195**

Farmers and food producers membership stickpin. **$85-$100**

Radio technician association, enamel pinback. **$75-$100**

Farmers association painted donation tinnie. **$45-$65**

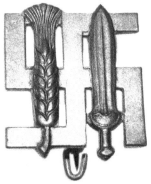

Farmers and food producers association membership pinback. **$75-$95**

1935 DAF supporter event tinnie, wood with stamped imprint on stickpin. **$45-$55**

Small animal breeders association membership stickpin. **$45-$65**

82

Meat and intestine inspectors guild membership stickpin in enamel. **$95-$125**

Aircraft industry merit award, enamel stickpin. **$185-$250**

Civil long service award stickpin. **$75-$95**

DAF cutout alloy membership stickpin with static swastika, RZM-marked. **$45-$65**

DAF/craft guild supporter stickpin on amber mount. **$125-$145**

NSBO membership stickpin. **$75-$100**

Stenographers guild enamel membership stickpin. **$75-$100**

Business association honor membership stickpin, enamel on silver. **$55-$75**

Business leaders organization enamel membership stickpin. **$75-$85**

Business association membership stickpin, enamel on silver. **$45-$65**

Business association membership stickpin, enamel on bronze. **$45-$65**

Business association membership stickpin, enamel on gilded metal. **$45-$65**

Hitlerjugend (HJ)

The NSDAP rode its ascension to power in Germany with the idea that it was a movement of and for the nation's youth, propelling Adolf Hitler into the chancellorship at 44 years of age.

Hitler had made note of Benito Mussolini's efforts using Italy's young men and women to promote his Fascist ideology in the 1920s, and understood that if similar programs could be utilized in Germany it would give the Nazi party a willing and obedient force to carry out anything that he required.

Germany had a long history of promoting youth groups, both religious and political, throughout the 19th and first part of the 20th century. Hitler began the first *Hitler Jungend* (HJ, Hitler Youth) group in 1925.

As the Nazis gained power, they incorporated other existing youth groups (*Stahlhelm, Hindenbergjungend, Jungsturm Kolberg*, Princess Louise, German Boy Scouts, and others) into their movement and designed a tightly ordered system to control the physical and mental education of each member.

The structure of the HJ separated Germany into *Obergebeit* (state districts) with smaller groups of *Gebeit, Banne, Unterbann, Stamm, Gefolschaft, Schar*, and *Kameradschaft* (10 boys). Hitler Youth were divided by gender and age into four major groups: Boys aged 10 to 14 were in the *Deutsches Jung Volk* (DJ, German Young People); boys 14-18 were in the *Hitler Jungen* (HJ, Hitler Youth); girls aged 10-14 were in the *Jungmadel* (JM, Young Girls); and girls 15-21 were in the *Bundes Deutscher Madel* (BDM, League of German Girls).

Membership in these groups was voluntary at first but became compulsory for all able-bodied youth as the war progressed. Boys in the DJ and HJ attended weekly meetings and participated in a series of activities that included sports (physical competitions leaning towards military field exercises), political indoctrination, and technical training. Camaraderie and the overall good of the group versus individual self-interest were stressed in these programs. Girls also attended weekly meetings, but these stressed political doctrines and homemaking

rather than physical abilities – in the Nazi culture, women were generally viewed as party members, mothers and wives first, though those positions changed in the later war years.

Boys and girls attended annual summer camps and national events geared toward building pride in the German nation and the Nazi movement. Handicapped youths could join special *Kameradschaften* where physical tests were altered to allow them to participate as fully acknowledged members.

HJ and DJ members wore a basic summer uniform of pullover light brown half-button shirt with a triangle in gold and black on the left sleeve designating the *Obergebeit/gebeit* to which they belonged. Below this could be worn their ranking or specialty patches (DJ members had a *sigrune*, a German rune for "victory" in the form of a single lightning bolt patch, below their triangle). Shoulder boards had color backing designating the wearer's branch of service (regular, flight, or naval) or (along with pips) level of leadership. Numbered buttons and embroidery designated their sub-districts. Hitler Youth membership enamel pins were worn on the left pocket, and proficiency badges and awards were worn on their respective sides according to the award's designation. A black leather belt with over-the-shoulder cross strap and buckle was worn, from which a *Fahrtmesser* (HJ traveling knife) could hang. A black wraparound scarf, leather neck slide, black shorts, socks and shoes completed the clothing for boys.

HJ teens wore an armband consisting of a black canted swastika in a white diamond over a red and white striped background. Early 1930s rank and file HJ wore a soft-visored tan cap with a round enamel sunrise HJ badge affixed to the front. This later changed to a tan overseas HJ cap with the diamond-shaped insignia in cloth. Winter uniforms featured dark blue wool long-sleeved jackets and long pants. Insignia were worn in the same manner as on summer uniforms. Wool-billed winter ski cap-style caps had enamel or cloth HJ emblems on the front. Marine HJ members wore uniforms and caps similar to those of the German navy, with HJ insignia in their respective positions. For sporting events, boys wore white tank top sports shirts with horizontal red stripes and HJ diamond insignias on the front with black shorts and sports shoes.

Adult male leaders of the HJ wore tan coats similar to those of political leaders, with dark slacks, white shirts, black ties, dark shoes, HJ armband, and tan visor cap fronted with HJ insignia.

The HJ membership badge started as an enameled party flag, then changed to a round enameled pin with sunburst and swastika with the words *"HJ Deutsche Arbeiter Jugend"* around the outside. In 1932, the final form was adopted: 24mm by 14mm diamond with red and white segments overlaid with a swastika in

the center. The DJ membership badge featured a silver *sigrune* on a red circle, overlaying a silver swastika on a black enamel background. The letters "DVJ" were printed on the face, but were later changed to "DJ." BDM members wore the same 1932 pattern HJ badge as male HJ members.

Marksmanship was a popular area in the HJ, and enamel shooting proficiency badges were awarded for course completion. The HJ badge featured silver crossed rifles on a black enameled circle overlaid with a red HJ diamond and swastika. The DJ award was similar, with a *sigrune* replacing the HJ emblem and the letters "D" and "J" on either side of the badge.

A series of proficiency badges were designed and awarded to those who passed tests in physical fitness and political astuteness. The HJ awards of iron, bronze, or silver featured a *Tyr-Rune* (German rune for "leadership in battle") overlaid with a swastika and the words *"Fur Leistungen in der HJ"* (for proficiency in the

HJ) in script along the outer edge. Most awards had an RZM (registered German manufacturer's code) mark and the recipient's serial number on the reverse. After a recipient left the HJ, he could continue to wear his award on his uniform as a member of the SA, SS, RAD, or the military service.

DJ badges were awarded in dull gray metal in the form of a *sigrune* overlaid with a swastika surrounded by the words *"Fur Leistungen Der DJ"* (for proficiency in the DJ). As with the HJ awards, RZM marks were usually on the reverse.

BDM members wore a tan suede-like jacket, *Kletterjacke* (climbing jacket), dark blue skirt, white blouse, black scarf with interwoven leather slides, socks, and shoes. District triangles in black and white were sewn to the left sleeves of blouses and jackets. Jacket sleeves also had striking cloth HJ diamonds sewn below the triangles. Enamel HJ membership pins were worn on the left breast pocket; proficiency badges and awards were worn on either side, depending on their individual designations. A beret was originally adopted at first, but later was dropped due to its unpopularity by the girls who wore them. In sporting competitions, girls wore the same white tops and black shorts as boys.

BDM and JM members could earn proficiency badges by passing tests centered on crafts, homemaking, and political indoctrination. The award featured a brass rectangle with a cutout "BDM or "JM" across the front. A red or red and white swatch of ribbon ran across the back and showed through the cutout sections. Many other badges were awarded and proudly worn by HJ members who excelled in sports, scholastics, technical abilities, or political indoctrination.

The organization, travel, and festivities promoted by the Hitler Youth helped children feel a sense of pride, well-being, and purpose after living through the economic depression and political uncertainty of post-World War I Germany. In 1940 there were over eight million members in the HJ. This enormous organization provided the Nazis with the young minds and bodies they needed to mold for their conquest of Europe. Millions of German army, navy, Luftwaffe, and SS personnel who fought and died for Hitler's Germany began their preparation for military service by being HJ members.

HJ summer overseas cap, tagged inside. **$325-$425**

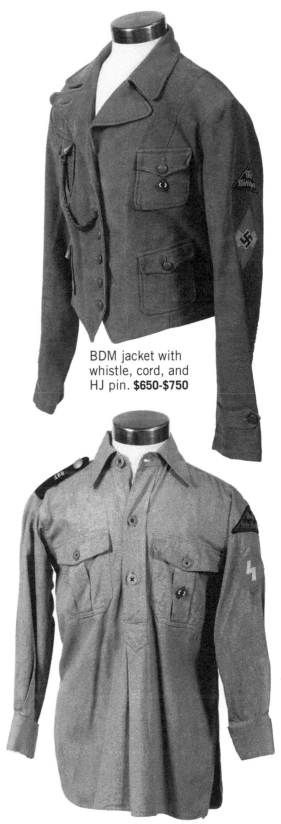

BDM jacket with whistle, cord, and HJ pin. **$650-$750**

HJ service shirt with scarf, slide, membership pin, armband, and lanyard. **$750-$850**

DJ service shirt with membership pin. **$375-$450**

HJ sports shirt. **$175-$250**

HJ flak helpers patch. **$75-$100**

HJ flieger patch. **$400-$475**

(Rick Fleury by JAG)

HJ section sleeve triangle. **$65-$95**

HJ marine shoulder boards. **$175-$225**

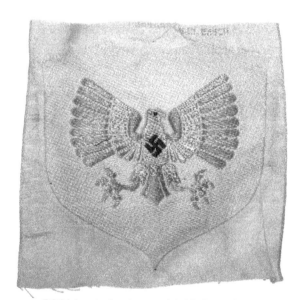

BDM leader's sleeve shield. **$125-$175**

HJ ranking chevron patch. **$35-$45**

DJ sleeve patch, tagged on reverse. **$45-$65**

HJ ranking pip sleeve patch. **$25-$35**

HJ ranking sleeve device. **$45-$55**

Standard HJ armband. **$75-$125**

Student league armband. **$150-$195**

HJ proficiency cloth badge for sports vest. **$75-$95**

Child-made party armband, GI acquired. **$75-$85**

HJ/BDM sleeve patch. **$85-$125**

Twenty-five-page HJ magazine supporting the war.
$65-$95

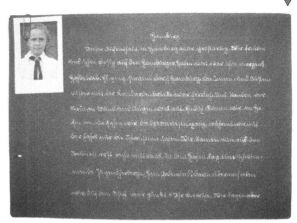

BDM girl with Sutterlin script prose. **$45-$55**

BDM membership and dues book. **$100-$150**

1934 German youth calendar and fact book. **$125-$150**

Munich school certificate. **$145-$175**

German insignia book for the HJ, stamped U.S. War Department copy. **$45-$75**

HJ group photo.

HJ lanyard and plastic whistle. **$125-$150**

HJ postcard. **$35-$45**

HJ buckle on variant belt made from plastic, maker-marked. **$450-$575**

DJ belt buckle. **$225-$275**

HJ made craft plaque. **$125-$175**

HJ painted buckle with variant catch system on reverse. **$150-$175**

HJ painted belt buckle. **$150-$175**

HJ traveling knife variant with motto, blued pommel cap, and crossguard. **$375-$425**

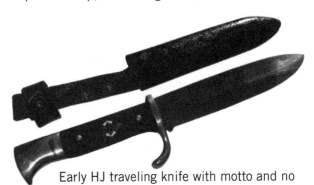

Early HJ traveling knife with motto and no ricasso. **$450-$650**

HJ nickel-plated parade belt buckle. **$225-$275**

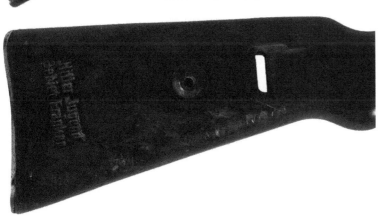

KKW .22 training rifle, butt stamped to Franken HJ section. **$950-$1,500**

HJ traveling knife in personalized scabbard with owner's 1925 date of birth and iron cross. **$450-$550**

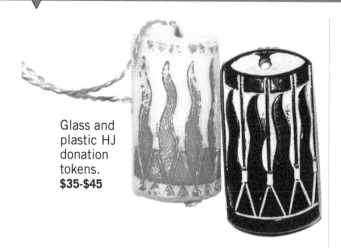

Glass and plastic HJ donation tokens. **$35-$45**

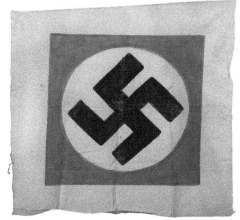

Home painted party flag on linen, taken from a German school. **$95-$125**

Winter relief donation tokens for the HJ. **$20-$35**

HJ command center pennant. **$285-$325**

BDM command pennants, 1-1/2 ft. x 2 ft. **$375-$450**

HJ banner, 4 ft. x 9 ft. **$450-$550**

HJ paper and candle party lantern. **$125-$150**

HJ golden leaders sports badge, numbered on reverse. **$450-$700**

1939 Austrian student world games badge, enamel. **$250-$275**

1935 HJ rally badge. **$35-$45**

HJ sharpshooter's badge, enamel, RZM-marked. **$185-$250**

Miniature golden leaders sports badge. **$195-$250**

Miniature HJ proficiency badge in bronze. **$65-$85**

Young horseman's badge in bronze. **$95-$125**

1938 county level HJ competition badge. **$325-$450**

DJ marksmanship badge, enamel. **$150-$185**

Westphalia regional HJ event badge. **$75-$85**

HJ proficiency badge in bronze. **$135-$175**

HJ proficiency badge in silver. **$175-$195**

1936 HJ rally badge. **$35-$45**

First version of the BDM proficiency badge with solid red ribbon. **$250-$350**

Final version of the BDM proficiency badge with striped ribbon. **$250-$350**

1940 HJ rally badge. **$35-$45**

1937 HJ rally badge. **$35-$45**

HJ marksmanship award, enamel, RZM-marked. **$135-$175**

DJ proficiency badge in gray metal. **$150-$185**

DJ support badge, cut-out tin. **$45-$55**

DJ membership pin, RZM-marked. **$125-$150**

NS university student organization pin, enamel. **$175-$225**

Final version of the HJ membership pin, enamel, RZM-marked. **$65-$85**

Golden HJ membership pin, serial numbered on reverse. **$275-$350**

1939 HJ sporting event pressed paper tinnie. **$55-$75**

Second version of the HJ pin, enamel. **$75-$100**

HJ membership pin, painted version, RZM-marked. **$55-$75**

1935 HJ Saar tinnie. **$75-$85**

BDM 1936 Franken sports day event tinnie. **$50-$75**

(Private Collection)

First version HJ membership pin, enamel. **$225-$275**

Youth national sports organization stickpin. **$100-$150**

DJ/HJ runic leather tinnie. **$35-$40**

1938 Swabian HJ sporting event tinnie. **$95-$125**

Student league organization membership pin, enamel, RZ-marked. **$125-$175**

1936 HJ Franken event tinnie. **$45-$65**

1934 HJ DAF bronze tinnie. **$125-$145**

Reichskriegerbund (RKB), Stahlhelm, Kyffhauser Bund, NSDMB

For many years German veterans' groups had aided ex-soldiers who needed economic help for themselves and their families, or who simply wanted to return to the camaraderie and order they experienced during their time in the armed forces. After the Treaty of Versailles, these groups grew exponentially as millions of soldiers found themselves out of the service in a defeated and economically devastated country.

To help stabilize the Weimar political scene in post-World War I, German veterans' groups began to rapidly change from social and economic havens to powerful paramilitary organizations spearheading political reform. Groups such as *Gruppe Reinhard, Bund Freikorps Epp*, and *Bund Oberland* formed private armies to show political might and to fight adversaries in the city streets, as often occurred.

In 1931 there were over three million members in thousands of local groups. Prewar group functions continued, but marksmanship instruction and other military training increased. In addition to retired soldiers' groups, women's and youth groups were created to allow entire families into respective memberships. German politicians wielded these groups in the changing political climate, and none was better at this than Adolf Hitler and the NSDAP.

With the Nazis' assumption of power, the main veterans' groups were the *Stahlhelm* (Steel Helmet), *Kyffhauser Bund* (National Associations of Veterans), *Reichstreubund* (Association of Faithful Former Professional Soldiers), *Soldantenbund* (Registered Soldiers League), and *NS Deutscher Marine-Bund* (NSDMB, National Socialist German Navy League). As the regime grew, many of these groups were consolidated into the *Reichskriegerbund* (RKB, German

National Association of Veterans) or became part of the SA – Storm Troopers. Because honoring both past and present military personnel was key in the Nazi philosophy, veterans' groups maintained and grew in social status throughout the Third Reich period, though they lost many members to rearmament programs.

During the "period of struggle" (1920s and 1930s), the Stahlhelm uniform consisted of a gray tunic and pants modeled after those worn by the field soldiers in World War I. Visored soft gray caps fronted a unique hollow back cap badge consisting of a nickel silver helmet profile, which went through a series of three changes. The first version featured a plain, rounded top helmet introduced in 1919. The second, introduced in 1920, was similar to the first type but with "Der Stahlhelm" added in script across the front. The third version was introduced in 1929 – an updated shape of helmet with the same text as the second version, and sometimes bearing a Maltese cross before the script, designating a frontline soldier. The badge had a rear pin attachment with a coiled wire catch. Frontline combatants also wore membership pins that consisted of a helmet profile in a circle of nickel silver with the letters "NSDFBSt" across the bottom.

The Stahlhelm was absorbed by the SA in 1933, at which time a Traditions badge was conceived. This badge consisted of a silver helmet on a 35mm black enamel round badge with the year of entry on the base. The badge reverse was engraved with the month, day, and year of the owner's entry into the Stahlhelm. Female members of the *Stahlhelm Frauenbundabzeichen* (auxiliary) wore a 22mm round badge with a silver "F" on top of an outlined helmet profile surrounded by midnight blue enamel. Stahlhelm youth members wore a silver sword pin with "Jung Stahlhelm" embossed across the front.

The Kyffhauser Bund had been in existence since 1871 and served to unite and help veterans from all different German states. The group's formal uniform of the 1930s consisted of a dark blue two-piece civilian-style suit on which were worn an armband and membership lapel pin, both containing the Kyffhauser insignia – a white oval divided with red on the lower third. The white field contained a black graduated tower on a raised mountaintop with a canted black swastika in a white circle at its base (pre-Nazi period emblems did not have the swastika beneath). Long-serving members were issued honor enamel membership pins with silver or gilded wreaths surrounding the borders and silver and black years of service circles on the top or bottom. Armbands were of dark blue wool with the colorful cloth Kyffhauser shield sewn in the center. Brocade stripes ran the length of the armband under the shield to designate higher ranks within the organization.

Members were allowed to wear their military and civilian awards in their respective positions on the tunic front. The uniform was topped with a dark blue civilian-style hard-brimmed visor cap with a cap band of alternating towers and swastikas in black, and a brass and enameled emblem on the front of the standard Kyffhauser emblem in an oval surrounded by a gilded wreath. Above this and below the crown was a roundel of the national colors. Flag bearers wore a beautiful silver and gilded gorget on a gilded chain when bearing the unit and national colors.

The Reichstreubund was formed during the Weimar period for the benefit of retired professional soldiers. Along with the Soldantenbund (formed in 1936), they dealt with social and economic problems for the soldiers, their families, and their widows. Both groups wore formal civilian-style suits like those of the Kyffhauser Bund, but with distinctly different group emblems. The Reichstreubund device was in the form of a swastika overlaid on a Maltese cross superimposed

over crossed swords. This was worn on a blue cap surrounded by an oak leaf and acorn wreath, or in either a stickpin or pinback silver and enamel membership pin worn on civilian clothing. The Soldantenbund emblem featured a nickel silver eagle mounted on crossed swords clutching a circular wreath with a swastika in its talons. In 1938 the RKB absorbed the Soldantenbund organization; the Reichstreubund continued as an independent entity to the end of the war.

The NSDMB for marine veterans was an older group that was renamed in 1935, became affiliated with the RKB until 1943, and then came under the direct command of the *Kriegsmarine* (German navy). As a rule this group did not wear a standard uniform, but some members did don dark blue suits during formal occasions, similar to suits worn by the RKB. The group did have specific regulations for caps and breast badges. The peaked caps with leather bills and chinstrap were similar to those worn by naval officers. A black mohair band surrounded the base, and a gilded wreath of oak leaves and acorns surrounding a roundel with the national colors was affixed to the front. Above this and below the rim was worn the NSDMB emblem consisting of a gilded eagle overlaying crossed swords and an anchor, a black Maltese cross on its chest, and an oak leaf circle with canted swastika clutched in its talons. A larger version of the same badge was worn as a breast eagle while on parade.

As the different veterans' groups were combined into the RKB, the official formal uniform was copied from the Kyffhauser Bund. The same dark blue suit and cap were worn, but the armband was replaced with one bearing the RKB emblem (or standard NSDAP armband). This emblem incorporated a red shield surrounding a Maltese cross with a canted swastika overlaid in a center circle. The breast badge consisted of an aluminum eagle with outstretched wings containing a Maltese cross overlaying swords on the front and clutching a wreath with a canted swastika. A miniature version of the badge was mounted on the upper front of the blue and black civilian-style cap, below which was mounted a silver oak leaf and acorn wreath surrounding a roundel with national colors. When in civilian clothes, RKB members could wear an enamel pinback or stickpin shield with the RKB emblem to show their affiliation. As with the Kyffhauser Bund, wreaths surrounded the honor badges of the RKB with years of service displayed in silver and black. RKB gorgets of elaborate silver, gilding and enamel, suspended with gilded chains of alternating links bearing swastikas and crosses, were worn by flag bearers during special occasions.

The twofold use of the veterans groups by the Nazi regime – first as part of a dominating force to defeat their enemies in political brawls, then as showpieces for public goodwill and advancement of the military – played a major role in the formation and acceptance of the Third Reich within German society. Because of lax restrictions, economic reasons, or defiant pride, some veterans wore their outdated insignia until the end of the war. The massive veteran membership and number of companies producing regalia for their use (in 1936 there were 539 companies authorized to make RKB caps alone) meant an abundance of membership pins, armbands, caps, and other insignia were always available for members to demonstrate their pride of time in service.

RKB visor cap. **$325-$450**

Kyffhauserbund visor cap. **$325-$450**

Naval veterans visor cap. **$65-$800**

Cloth variant RKB breast eagle. **$225-$275**

(Private Collection)

Early or pre-Nazi Kyffhauserbund membership patch. **$25-$35**

Kyffhauserbund mid-level armband. **$125-$145**

RKB mid-level armband. **$135-$165**

RKB basic armband. **$85-$125**

Front Heil veteran's buckle, brass. **$175-$225**

Reichstreubund enamel emblem. **$65-$85**

RKB flag bearer's gorget with chain. **$775-$900**

Stahlhelm membership identity booklet. **$125-$175**

Early or pre-Nazi Kyffhauserbund membership card. **$45-$55**

Imperial German flag used by many veterans groups, 1.5 ft. x 2 ft. **$125-$175**

Soldatenbund identification membership book. **$125-$175**

Soldatenbund table banner, 1.25 ft. x 1.5 ft. **$450-$500**

Flag for the Soldatenbund, career veterans, 3.3 ft. x 3.5 ft. **$450-$575**

Ribbon bar for Hindenburg cross for combatants. **$30-$35**

Ribbon bar with Imperial awards and Hindenburg cross. **$45-$65**

Six-place medal bar with Hindenburg combatants cross and Imperial and Nazi medals. **$350-$400**

(Private Collection)

Four-place medal bar with Imperial awards and Hindenburg cross. **$175-$225**

Hindenburg cross on salesman's sample card. **$65-$85**

Four-place civilian-mount medal bar with Hindenburg cross and Imperial medals. **$275-$325**

(Private Collection)

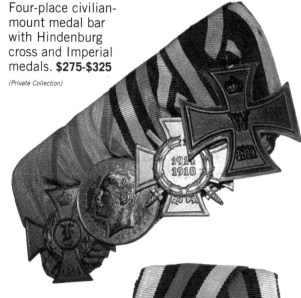

Hindenburg medal in parade mount. **$65-$75**

Medal bar with iron cross and Hindenburg World War I combatants medal. **$135-$165**

Hindenburg cross for combatants. **$45-$55**

Hindenburg cross for World War I non-combatants. **$35-$45**

Hindenburg cross for widows, parents and orphans of slain World War I soldiers. **$85-$100**

World War I veterans commemorative medal. **$45-$55**

Veterans league service medal and ribbon. **$85-$100**

Early or pre-Nazi Kyffhauserbund cap badge and wreath. **$50-$60**

RKB cap badge with prongs. **$65-$85**

Kyffhauser cap badge. **$45-$65**

Navy veterans league cap eagle. **$85-$100**

Early or pre-Nazi Kyffhauserbund cap insignia, enamel. **$65-$85**

RKB membership breast eagle. **$75-$95**

Kyffhauserbund cap badge and wreath. **$45-$75**

RKB unfinished breast eagles.
$45-$55

RKB aluminum breast eagle with painted cross. **$75-$85**

Navy veterans league breast eagle.
$125-$150

NSKOV membership badge.
$65-$75

NSKOV gilded membership badge. **$75-$85**

NSKOV marksmanship award badge. **$85-$95**

Alpine Kyffhauserbund badge, enamel center. **$95-$125**

NSKOV honor badge, enamel and gild. **$275-$325**

1926 Stahlhelm members commemorative badge, inscription on reverse. **$275-$325**

Kyffhauserbund honor badge for armband. **$95-$125**

Stahlhelm membership combatant's pin with cross. **$45-$75**

Stahlhelm commemorative civilian-wear badge. **$150-$200**

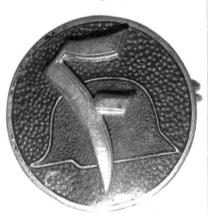

Stahlhelm women's auxiliary membership badge, enamel. **$200-$300**

Stahlhelm membership combatant's pin. **$100-$125**

Stahlhelm youth membership pin. **$125-$150**

RKB 50-year service pin, enamel. **$150-$175**

RKB 25-year service pin, enamel. **$85-$100**

RKB 40-year service pin, enamel. **$100-$135**

Twenty-five-year Kyffhauserbund service pin, enamel. **$85-$100**

Early or pre-Nazi period Kyffhauserbund 25-year service pin, enamel. **$75-$95**

Kyffhauserbund membership pin. **$45-$65**

German cavalry veterans association pin. **$125-$175**

Disabled Veterans group membership pin, enamel. **$125-$150**

Early or pre-Nazi period Kyffhauserbund membership pin. **$35-$45**

1935 Gau Treffen Stahlhelm tinnie. **$125-$150**

Kyffhauserbund shooting award pin. **$100-$125**

(Private Collection)

Veterans day tinnie. **$45-$55**

(Private Collection)

Veterans early event tinnie. **$55-$65**

RKB tinnie. **$35-$45**

NSKOV event tinnie, bronze. **$75-$85**

1938 Calvary veterans group meeting tinnie. **$45-$55**

Group Ehrhardt, early veterans paramilitary group membership stickpin, enamel. **$250-$300**

RKB miniature membership eagle stickpin. **$45-$65**

Stickpin with iron cross and Hindenburg World War I combatants cross. **$45-$65**

Hindenburg cross miniature stickpin. **$35-$45**

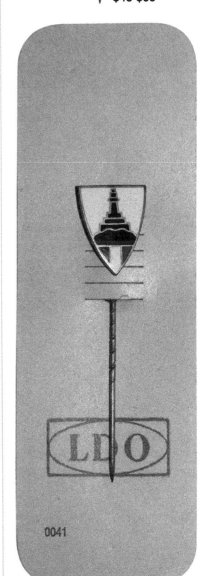

RKB membership enamel stickpin. **$55-$75**

Veteran of the Kings Imperial guard stickpin. **$75-$95**

Early or pre-Nazi unissued Kyffhauserbund pin on LDO card. **$75-$85**

Schutzstaffel
(SS)

In the early years of struggle for political dominance, Adolf Hitler ordered a small group of his most trusted men be organized into a personal bodyguard for himself and other high-profile members of the NSDAP. This resulted in the corps of the Fuhrer's bodyguards dressed in black uniforms with silver accents and red armbands – the dark knights of the Nazi regime.

No other followers of Adolf Hitler's Third Reich epitomized blind loyalty to the State's leader, fanatical sacrifice in the fields of battle, and inhuman depths of moral depravity to which an otherwise normal group of individuals could sink than members of the *Schutzstaffel*, the SS. The brown, black, gray, and field green-clad members were revered as heroes by their fellow "racially pure" citizens, but were feared by others considered inferior in the Nazi regime. By terrorizing and murdering millions of innocent people, Hitler's SS men wrote one the most sinister chapters in German history.

In 1923 a small contingency of personal guards was formed, and by 1925 was named the *Schutzstaffel der NSDAP* (protection squad of the Nazi party). This group of guards remained small and singularly purposed until a new SS leader, Heinrich Himmler, was appointed in 1927. With Himmler at the helm, the SS grew into the most powerful force within the Nazi party, slowly encroaching on many political, legal, and military entities of the Reich and finally exceeding 1.25 million members by the end of the war.

The organization of the SS went through many changes during its exponential growth, with the last divisions consisting of the *Allgemeine* (general) and *Waffen* (armed) SS. SS men were initially chosen for service after rigorous racial, ethnic, and physical testing. For instance, officer candidates had to prove they came from pure "Aryan" descendents going back to the year 1750. Once accepted into the program, new recruits were trained for 20 weeks in physical endurance, military skills, and political indoctrination with emphasis on unit camaraderie and adherence to Nazi philosophies.

With Hitler's ascension to power in 1933, SS men were assigned to the new concentration camps as guards of political prisoners and other "undesirables" of the Nazi regime. A personal pledge of loyalty to Adolf Hitler and his ideals was key in the development of SS men, who terrorized many citizens in the country and became the instruments of the "final solution" – elimination of all unwanted people in lands to be claimed by the Reich.

Waffen SS units were at first comprised of German volunteers, but as the war progressed and their numbers were decimated, foreign legions of SS men were raised to help defeat the Russian Bolsheviks. Well-equipped and effectively used as fighting units in the war fronts, the Waffen SS became legendary as excessively aggressive soldiers who often fought to the death. Unfortunately, behind these warriors came the SS *Einsatzgruppen* (task forces) who rounded up many of the original inhabitants, especially Jews and Slavs in Eastern countries, for mass extermination.

Early Allgemeine SS wore heavy, brown long-sleeved shirts like those of the SA, with black ties, black riding breeches, black boots, and black belts with cross straps and silver buckles. This uniform was topped off with a distinctive black "coffee can" cap bearing a death's-head insignia (skull and crossbones) and national eagle, wreath, and swastika. Belt buckles were silver-toned, rectangular in shape for enlisted men and round for officers. In the center of each buckle was an eagle (straight-winged on enlisted and downswept rounded on officer) perched on an oak leaf wreath containing a static swastika. Around the wreath were the words *"Meine Ehre heisst Treue"* (my honor is loyalty) stamped into the surface. A red armband with white circle, black border stripes, and black swastika was worn on the left arm in addition to the NSDAP party pin on the shirt breast or pinned to the tie front.

As SS men took on additional responsibilities within the party, their uniforms changed. Black tunics with white collar piping were added to the traditional brown shirts. Patches were worn on tunic collars with a series of embroidered, metal, or bullion cords, *siegrune* (runic lightning bolts, the sign of the SS) pips, and oak leaves to designate the wearer's rank. Political or military awards could be worn in their respective places on the front panels of the tunic while cuff titles were often affixed to the lower left sleeve to indicate unit affiliation. Black visor caps with white piping and black leather or fiber visors replaced the coffee can caps. A stylized death's-head symbol was pinned on the front of the hatband; above it rested a straight-winged eagle perched on an oak leaf circle surrounding a canted swastika. Some higher-ranking SS leaders wore variant uniforms and caps in the same design as those of the black-clad members, but in dark gray colors. A summer version was also later introduced, which featured all-white tunics and caps.

Wearing the Allgemeine uniform became strictly limited when the war broke out, with many of the black uniforms turned in to SS depots so that they could be reissued to Nazi groups in foreign countries.

Dress daggers were worn for walking out or on formal occasions. The 1933 model for officers and enlisted men was fashioned after the SA dagger of a Swiss 16th century hunting knife. The SS dagger had a black ebony or dyed wood handle with a silver eagle, wreath, and swastika embedded in the center of the handle. A black enamel disk with double siegrunen was inlaid above this. The polished twin-edged blade bore the same motto as the belt buckle, *"Meine Ehre heisst Treue."* The crossguard and pommel were elongated nickel silver (plated on later models), while the scabbard was anodized black with nickel throat and toe (painted body with plated accents on later models). The dagger hung from either a single leather buckled strap or a two-piece vertical marching hanger. In 1936, the officer's dagger was changed with the addition of a permanently fixed silver-linked hanger that featured alternating skulls and

siegrunes on the links.

The officer's SS sword had a slender silver blade mounted with a silver wire-wrapped black, slightly bulbous handle. The handle base was capped by an oak leaf ferule that supported the bottom of a thin "D" guard that wrapped around to a plain pommel cap. The officer's model contained a siegrune emblem on a round base inlaid into the center of the handle, while the candidate's model featured a plain handle with siegrunen on the pommel cap. The sword was mounted in a black straight-metal scabbard with silver swirl-patterned throat and drag. A single silver suspension ring accommodated a belt hanger.

SS men proudly exhibited their membership with a double siegrune black-on-white round patch worn on their sports vests when competing in sporting events. When not in uniform, an SS man wore a black and silver round siegrune enamel stickpin on his civilian coat lapel. Men who had served with the SS for long periods of time were presented with long service medals and ribbon bars for four, eight, 12, and 25 years. Additional years were counted for times in military service or the police, as well as extra time for early members.

In 1934, Heinrich Himmler began presenting SS rings to selected members for loyalty to the organization. These highly coveted round silver rings bore a series of runic symbols around the outer edges with a predominant death's-head symbol on the front.

The Waffen SS uniform presented a more typical military appearance, attempting to duplicate the gray-green uniforms of the regular army. Tunics were made of wool (with finer fabric for officers) with dark green collars to which ranking tabs were attached. In addition, a cloth or bullion SS eagle and swastika wreath was sewn onto the left upper sleeve, with ranking arm chevrons and shoulder boards added to make the uniforms more closely resemble those of the army. Like other members of the *Wehrmacht* (armed service), military awards were worn on the front panels of Waffen SS tunics.

Other variations of the armed SS attire included a black SS panzer corps "wrapper" (short jacket designed to overlap in the front and button at the side) and an open-collared tunic preferred by administrative personnel. Visor caps of gray-green material and insignia similar to the black caps of the general SS were worn, along with army-type overseas caps in the same green material as the tunics. These featured a death's-head cloth emblem sewn to the front rim with an SS eagle, wreath, and swastika sewn above. Variations were made of black material with a cloth SS eagle sewn to the side and a silver death's-head button affixed to the front rim.

When massive casualties began to take their toll on the Waffen SS at the Eastern Front, numerous divisions were recruited from Germany's allies. Many of these new, non-German groups wore their own patches to identify their units and nationalities. In addition, some foreign members wore ethnically shaped caps, such as the brimless fez worn by the Croatian *Handschar* division, which allowed the Muslim wearer to press his forehead to a prayer rug.

Women auxiliaries participated in the SS, with most serving in clerical capacities, freeing their male counterparts for active military service. A few female members became notorious for their cruelty to inmates of the Nazi concentration camps to which they were posted. These women were severely punished after the war.

The SS was disbanded by the occupying Allies in 1945. Although many of the Waffen SS fought gallantly as elite soldiers of their homeland, many other Allgemeine and Waffen members were found guilty of the atrocities they committed before and during the war. Because of their ferocity in battle and their image as the darkest of enemies, scores of Allied soldiers attempted to collect items of the SS as the war in Europe came to a close. In addition, with their defeat, countless SS personnel destroyed their uniforms and attempted to blend back into the general population to escape retribution. These practices, along with the general rigors of time, have limited the supply of original SS memorabilia in today's collecting market.

Allgemeine SS service kepi. **$3,000-$10,000**

(Private Collection)

Allgemeine SS officer's visor cap. **$4,500-$6,500**

(JAG)

Variant Allgemeine SS guard's helmet. **$1,800-$2,500**

Waffen SS Handschar division officer's fez. **$950-$1,200**

Waffen SS sergeant's tunic, Totenkopf division, with shooting lanyard, ribbon bar, party pin, rider's badge, and war merit service cross. **$8,500-$9,500**

SS sports vest patches, paper RZM tag. **$250-$265** Cloth RZM tag. **$275-$300**

SS embroidered edelweiss patch. **$95-$125**

SS tropical cloth ranking pip. **$35-$40**

SS tropical rank chevron. **$45-$55**

Waffen SS volunteer Horst Wessel collar tab.
$150-$175

SS enlisted collar tab.
$450-$500

SS old fighter chevron. **$85-$125**

Enlisted SS shoulder eagle. **$125-$150**

(Rick Fleury)

SS multi-piece armband. **$450-$600**

SS enlisted belt buckle, RZM-marked. **$500-$650**

SS armband with cloth RZM tags on reverse.
$650-$800

Waffen SS enlisted belt buckle, RZM-marked, green
paint remaining on reverse. **$450-$600**

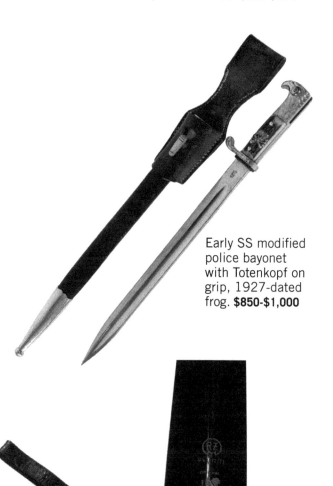

Early SS modified
police bayonet
with Totenkopf on
grip, 1927-dated
frog. **$850-$1,000**

Eickhorn transitional model
33 SS dagger with vertical
hanging strap. **$3,900-$4,500**

(Chris DePere)

Model 1933 Robert Klaas maker-marked SS dagger with vertical hanging strap. **$3,900-$4,500**

Winter relief token, SS plastic man. **$35-$50**

Death's-head private purchase ring, GI-captured. **$350-$450**

SS death's-head ring. **$4,500-$7,000**

(JAG)

Death's-head enamel private purchase SS cufflink. **$450-$600**

Waffen SS typewriter with SS 5-key, in case. **$750-$1,000**

SS ausweis. **$450-$600**

SS Totenkopf man postcards. **$65-$85**

SS and police color postcard. **$65-$85**

SS death memorial card with Christian prayer on reverse. **$45-$65**

SS four-year service medal. **450-$600**

Ten-place ribbon bar with two SS long service awards. **$425-$450**

Nine-place ribbon bar with SS long service, Imperial, and Nazi awards. **$450-$550**

Early SS death's-head cap emblem with prongs. **$450-$550**

SS eight-year service medal. **750-$900**

SS cap eagle with prongs, RZM-marked. **$650-$800**

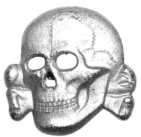

SS death's-head cap emblem, painted with prongs, RZM-marked. **$650-$800**

SS four-year service medal with full original black paint. **$450-$650**

Early NSDAP/ SS cap eagle with prongs. **$50-$75**

Belgium SS sponsor membership lapel pin, enamel, Antwerp-marked. **$450-$550**

SS death's-head cap emblem with prongs, RZM-marked. **$750-$900**

SS sponsor's stickpin, enamel. **$375-$450**

Deutsches Heer

The most extensive element of the Wehrmacht that fulfilled the manpower requirements of the Nazi war machine was the *Deutsches Heer* (German Army). During his public career, Adolf Hitler first served, then feared, courted, and finally commanded what was to become one of the greatest military forces of the 20th century.

Though adhering to much of the old disciplinary principles of the Imperial Army, the army under the NSDAP was well-equipped with the best technology of the time and its soldiers well-taught in the tactics of combat. As the supreme commander, Hitler demonstrated an extreme ambivalence toward the soldiers of the Reich, publicly praising them for their acts of valor one moment and then needlessly condemning thousands to their deaths without giving much thought to their fate the next moment. If Hitler had realized his own limitations and allowed more leeway to the general officers of the German high command, the outcome of the European war may well have ended much differently than it did.

Following the massive defeat of Imperial Germany in 1918, the Treaty of Versailles limited the new *Reichswehr* (defense force) to 100,000 men, a small amount of armor, and no aircraft. Many paramilitary groups across Germany, including the NSDAP's SA brown shirts, began clandestine training for self-defense and to take control of the government if given the chance. Thousands of men and youths were trained in military drill, firearms, field strategy, and other combat skills. When the Nazi party assumed control in 1933, the new central government continued to train and rebuild the German Army. Hitler publicly ignored the Allies Treaty and openly began a massive rearmament program, bringing back conscription in the spring of 1935. In 1936 the first actual test of the new military's abilities came about when Hitler sent air force and armored troops to help Franco achieve victory in the Spanish Civil War.

In September 1939, the Army, along with the other branches of the German Wehrmacht, made the fateful push into Poland, beginning the European campaign.

The Heer was comprised of a large variety of specialty services including infantry, artillery, panzer, pioneer, supply, smoke, machine gun, motorcycle, medical, transport, mountain troops, administrative, and military police, among others. These divisions, along with other service branches, worked in coordination to optimize the military strength, support, and effectiveness of their troops.

Army ranks included more than 20 separate ratings beginning with the *Schutze* (private) and ending with the *Generalfeldmarschall* (field marshal). There were also ranks specific to a specialty of service, such as a *Santitatsobergefreiter* (medical corps corporal) or a *Feldbischof* (brigadier general chaplain).

In addition, the army contained sections of *Wehrmachtbeamten* (non-soldier administrative personnel) who dressed in uniform but were not considered by the German military to be actual combat personnel.

By 1939 – after going through a series of changes, the final in 1944 with a short, cheapened model of jacket – the basic enlisted soldier's tunic consisted of mid-length dress for formal occasions or field model for combat wear.

Dress uniforms were made of gray-green wool with dark green collars and eight silver buttons on the front. Silver buttons were also attached to the shoulder straps and on the reverse of the tunic as belt ramps and tail decoration; pockets were hidden inside the coattails. Piping to designate branch of service (white for infantry, red for artillery, black for pioneer, blue for medical, etc.) was sewn down the front seam and along the rear tails. Cuffs were covered with dark green material, mounted with bullion rectangles, and had additional buttons. A silver and green national insignia of an eagle with outstretched wings perched on an oak leaf circle in the center of which sat a rotated swastika (*Reichsadler*) was sewn to the right upper breast panel. Medals or other military awards could be worn on their respective positions on the front panels of the tunic. Matching wool pants, black boots, and a belt and buckle finished the main body. The buckle was rectangular (round for officers) and contained a closed-wing eagle holding a rotated swastika in two concentric circles containing a half wreath of oak leaves on the bottom half. Around the upper half of the inner circle was stamped *"Gott Mit Uns"* (God with us). A standard German helmet with (and later without) national color shield and army eagle decals completed the attire. In addition to helmets, visor caps with green bodies, black leather visors, black chinstraps, and branch of service piping were also worn. On the front cap band was affixed an oak leaf wreath

with a cockade containing the national colors of red and black in a silver base. Above this was pinned an eagle perched on a round oak leaf wreath surrounding a canted swastika. A double-bar collar insignia was surrounded with silver *litzen* (lace – thick piping) for NCOs, and rank was designated by a series of shoulder boards, pips, and chevrons.

Combat uniforms were made of courser, more durable material with five subdued buttons. They lacked the ornate cuffs, collars, and service piping used on the front and rear of the dress tunics. Upper and lower pockets were added to carry equipment, and a bandage pocket was sewn into the lower front liner. Heavy pants or riding britches, boots, and field gear (canteen, bread bag, rucksack, etc.) completed the soldier's field attire. Twin sets of black closed-cover ammo pouches were often worn on the belt to hold bullets for the primary infantry rifle, the Karabiner 98 (K-98). Soldiers wore visorless field caps of matching materials with the national cockade and eagle sewn to the front. Certain military decorations could be worn, such as 1st Class iron crosses and wound badges, but fully ribboned

medals were replaced with ribbon bars for fieldwear. A long gray-green wool field coat was worn during inclement weather, with or without a belt around the outer waist.

When walking out or on parade, dress bayonets could be worn to accent a uniform. These often consisted of plated or high polish single-edged blades with simple nickel crossguards, backstraps, and bird's-head pommels. Black plastic crosshatched or stag-handled grips were riveted in place. Bayonets were carried in black painted scabbards mounted in black leather suspension frogs that attached to the belt. Many variations of dress daggers were produced, including etched or engraved blades and shortened models for NCOs. Most often a cloth and bullion portepeed was wrapped around the upper portion of the belt frog to designate the owner's unit.

An officer's dress uniform was constructed of finer material than that of an enlisted man's, and often was custom-tailored. Gabardine replaced wool, and the insignias were handmade of bullion thread rather than the plainer cotton and silver wire. Brocade silver and green belts with highly polished round buckles were worn when on parade. Officers' bullion collar tabs and assorted shoulder boards demonstrated rank.

Officers could carry army daggers when walking out or on special occasions. An officer's dagger featured a polished double-edged plain blade (though etched or engraved models were available to the purchaser) mounted with a spiraled celluloid handle that ranged in color from white to dark orange. The silver crossguard showed a spread-winged eagle clutching an oak leaf wreath around a canted swastika; the ends were turned to form down-curled loops. A silver pommel cap in an inverted cone shape was decorated with sprigs of oak leaves and had a smooth dome top. A pebbled scabbard was held in place by two suspension rings decorated with oak leaves and a plain polished toe.

Officers could also carry full swords on special occasions. German army swords came in a variety of different designs depending on the owner's preference and pocketbook. Common types included the dove's-head and lion's-head styles. The dove's-head style typically consisted of a one-edged, slightly curved slender polished blade ending in an ornately carved gilt "D" guard with rounded top and backstrap. Crossguards had a variation of eagle, wreath, and swastika with a plain langet on the reverse. The sword rested in a black-painted single hanger scabbard made of steel. Lion's-head sabers were similar to dove's-head with the exception of the top pommel area, which was molded into the design of a lion's head with red cut crystal gemstones in the eye sockets. These and other types of officers' swords were wrapped with leather and silver wire portepeeds. Besides the swords produced during the Third Reich, senior officers often carried their honored Imperial German swords during dress occasions.

Officers' field tunics were designed without dark cuffs and seam piping, and with only five buttons, but the materials and quality were similar to parade models. Riding britches and boots were the preferred accompaniment to tunics, over which were worn brown belts with double-claw silver buckles. Officers' visor caps were of superior quality with lighter color materials, silver bullion cord chinstraps, and high polish metal or bullion cap badges. Field caps were also of better-quality material with bullion insignia and silver piping around the upper fold. Field equipment for officers was at a minimum, with small-caliber holstered sidearms and map cases the most prevalent items carried. The insignia on the uniforms and caps of general officers was of gilt rather than the silver thread found on lower ranks. Like enlisted men, officers wore long gray-green material or leather coats during inclement weather. Shoulder boards showed the wearer's rank.

Other branches of the army had specialty uniforms specific to their duties, such as panzer units. Besides standard tunics with pink-lined shoulder boards and collar tabs, panzer gun crews wore "wraps" – black, close-fitting, broad-lapelled tunics with front buttons mounted to the side. These were worn with loose-fitting trousers, low boots, and black caps (first a beret, later an overseas cap). *Sturmgeschutz* (assault gun) crews wore the same style of uniform but with dark gray-green rather than black fabric. *Behelfspersonal* (women army auxiliaries), who often worked in clerical and other support positions, dressed in gray-green tunics with matching skirts and overseas caps.

Many military awards were originally developed by the army for its members, such as the *Infanterie-Sturmabzeichen* (infantry assault badge), *Panzerk Ampfabzeichen* (tank battle badge), *Allgemeines Sturmabzeichen* (general assault badge), and *Nahkampfspange* (close combat bar). As the war progressed, these badges were awarded to other branches of the Wehrmacht if service-specific alternative badges did not already exist.

In 1933, most countries in Europe, still reeling from the effects of the Great War and a flimsy pact made with Russia and the isolationist United States, allowed the new German government to actively pursue their military goals. With the success of the Austrian, Memel, and Czech Anschlusses, Hitler's army prepared to conquer Europe, putting them under his tyrannical boot. Though over 13 million German soldiers fought valiantly for the honor, tradition, and defense of their homeland and people, in the end their efforts would only be remembered for the evil dictator they represented.

Artillery enlisted visor cap. **$425-$550**

Pioneer enlisted visor cap. **$525-$650**

Infantry officer's fine-quality visor cap. **$675-$875**

Infantry enlisted visor cap. **$425-$550**

Administration visor cap. **$475-$625**

Cork-based tropical pith helmet. **$325-$425**

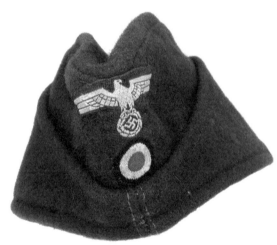
Quality private-purchase enlisted overseas cap.
$325-$450

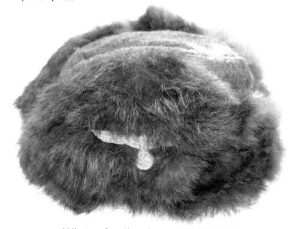
Winter fur-lined cap. **$275-$425**

Child's toy army helmet with cloth liner and chinstrap. **$475-$675**

(Chris Depere)

Artillery NCO tunic with shooting lanyard and silver wound badge, ribbons in buttonhole. **$875-$1,100**

1935 single-decal helmet. **$450-$575**

1918 transitional single-decal helmet. **$650-$750**

Infantry officer's tunic with gold wound badge, ribbon bar, and iron cross. **$1,200-$1,350**

Administrative mid-level officer's tunic with horseman's badge, ribbon bar, iron cross and wound badge. **$1,250-$1,400**

Pants for administrative officer's uniform. **$250-$300**

Africa Corps cuff title. **$275-$350**

Artillery officer's tunic with infantry assault badge, ribbon bar, and field visor. **$750-$1,100**

Calvary dress tunic cuff and collar tab set. **$125-$175**
(Private Collection)

Officer's panzer breast eagle. **$125-$175**

Enlisted wire thread breast eagle. **$45-$65**

Panzer ranking chevron. **$45-$55**

Late war breast eagle. **$45-$50**

Late war cap eagle. **$35-$45**

Tank destruction sleeve badge. **$475-$575**

Army sports vest eagle. **$65-$85**

Officer candidate armband. **$325-$375**

Stretcher barrier armband. **$125-$150**

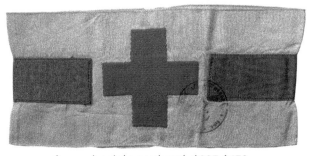

Army chaplain armband. **$325-$450**

Service of the armed forces armband. **$95-$135**

Army parade steward armband. **$145-$175**

Armed forces worker armband. **$95-$135**

Armored mechanic sleeve badge. **$75-$95**
(Private Collection)

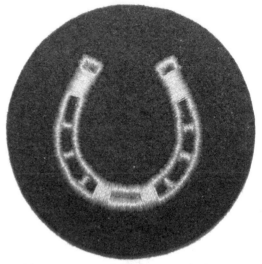

Liveryman specialty arm patch. **$20-$25**

Georgian foreign volunteer patch. **$65-$75**

Jager arm patch. **$45-$65**

Signals specialty arm patch. **$20-$25**

Artillery gun layer specialty patch. **$25-$30**

Foreign volunteer arm patches. **$45-$65**

(Chris DePere)

Early army sports vest patch. **$75-$85**

First grade shooting lanyard. **$125-$145**

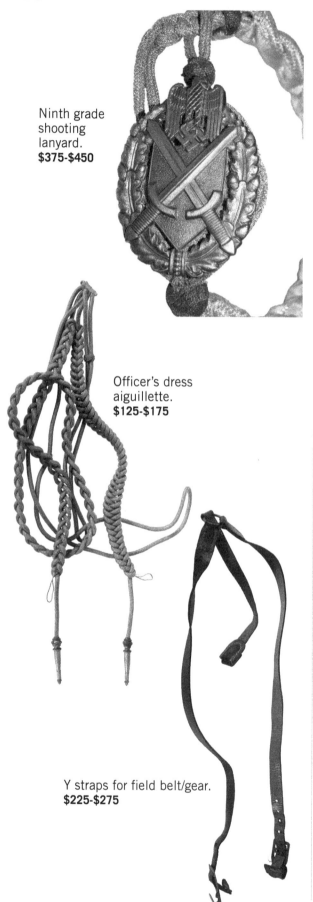

Ninth grade shooting lanyard. **$375-$450**

Officer's dress aiguillette. **$125-$175**

Y straps for field belt/gear. **$225-$275**

Unissued enlisted soldier's field belt and buckle. **$350-$450**

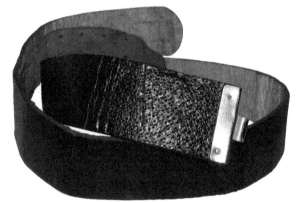

Paper ersatz belt. **$75-$90**

Enlisted man's buckle, early or pre-Nazi Reichswehr. **$125-$150**

Enlisted man's field buckle. **$125-$175**

Weapons

Weapons of the Third Reich were shared among all the military, and, if required, civilian workers and paramilitary forces. Smaller handguns were popular among soldiers who worked in confined spaces, such as aviators and armored vehicle personnel. Police detectives, bankers, and others who relied on concealed weapons for their work also favored "pocket pistols." Because the Heer was the largest armed force during the Nazi regime, examples interchanged by all segments of the Reich are listed in this section.

Byf 44 P38 semi-automatic 9mm pistol. **$650-$1,000**
(Chris Depere)

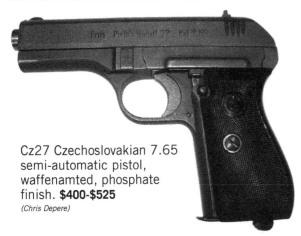

Cz27 Czechoslovakian 7.65 semi-automatic pistol, waffenamted, phosphate finish. **$400-$525**
(Chris Depere)

Spanish Astra 600 7.65 mm, waffenamted. **$450-$600**
(Chris Depere)

Spreewerks P38 standard service pistol with rough finishing. **$650-$1,500**

Mauser 1934 semi-automatic pistol, 7.65mm, waffenamted. **$450-$600**
(Chris Depere)

Belgium Browning model 22 7.65mm semi-automatic pistol, waffenamted. **$450-$650**
(Chris Depere)

Hungarian P37 7.65mm semi-automatic pistol, waffenamted. **$450-$750**
(Chris Depere)

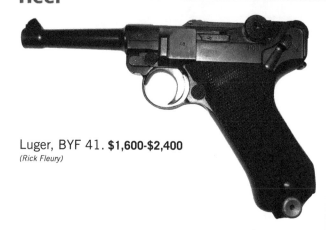

Luger, BYF 41. **$1,600-$2,400**
(Rick Fleury)

Aluminum frame flare
pistol. **$375-$550**

Early three-lever slotted Polish
P35 Radom 9mm semi-
automatic pistol. **$1,000-$1,400**
(Chris Depere)

M42 flare pistol with
Bakelite grips. **$325-$475**

Czechoslovakian P39
9mm semi-automatic
pistol. **$575-$675**

Late-war Polish Radom
semi-automatic 9mm
pistol. **$650-$800**

Saur 38H 7.65mm semi-
automatic pistol. **$650-$775**

Cz27 high polish
7.65mm semi-automatic
pistol, waffenamted.
$675-$850

Walther PPK 22 cal. pistol with extend magazine.
$750-$1,000
(Chris Depere)

Walther HSC 7.65mm semi-automatic pistol, waffenamted. **$450-$600**
(Chris Depere)

K-98 rifle with sling and front sight cover, Heer-marked in the butt stock.
$650-$1,100

660 Steyr-made K-98 rifle with sling, Heer-marked in the butt stock.
$850-$1,200

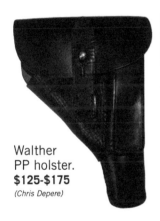

Walther PP holster.
$125-$175
(Chris Depere)

Luger holster with extra mag.
$375-$475
(Rick Fleury)

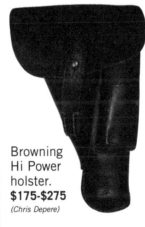

Browning Hi Power holster.
$175-$275
(Chris Depere)

Polish P35 Radom holster.
$175-$300
(Chris Depere)

P38 hard-shell holster. **$275-$375**
(Chris Depere)

P39 holster for Czech 39 pistol. **$275-$375**

Browning Model 22 drop holster. **$225-$325**
(Chris Depere)

Cz27 flap holster.
$125-$150

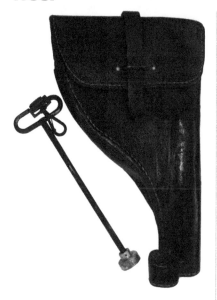

Paper and leather holster with cleaning rod for flare pistol, waffenamted in flap. **$375-$450**

Mauser 1934 holster with belt loop added to the toe. **$150-$200**
(Chris Depere)

Hungarian P37 drop holster. **$275-$350**
(Chris Depere)

Dove's-head officer's dress sword with open-wing eagle. **$400-$65**

Dove's-head engraved handle officer's dress sword. **$450-$650**

Dove's-head officer's dress sword with closed-wing eagle. **$450-$650**

Lion's-head officer's dress sword with triple-engraved blade. **$1,100-$1,450**

Robert Klaas lion's-head dress sword with hanger and portepeed. **$675-$850**

Army dagger with hangers, maker-marked. **$650-$800**

Stag-handled NCO clip point dress bayonet with portepeed. **$375-$450**

Miniature dress bayonet with portepeed. **$250-$325**

Army officer's dagger with double engraved blade and hangers, maker-marked. **$1,750-$2,500**

Enlisted soldier's stag-handled long parade bayonet. **$350-$425**

Miniature dress bayonet with eagle etched blade. **$350-$425**

Puma trench knife. **$425-$575**

Enlisted soldier's dress bayonet with engraved blade, frog, and portepeed. **$425-$650**

Set of two rifle ammunition belt pouches. **$75-$90**

9mm training bullets. **$25-$35**

8mm rifle training bullet. **$10-$15**

"Spork" spoon and fork field utensil. **$45-$65**

Personal camp stove with fuel pellet. **$45-$65**

Standard canteen and aluminum cup. **$95-$125**

Officer's small tropical canteen with Bakelite cup. **$175-$250**

10 x 50 binoculars with eye lens covers, case, and strap. **$375-$475**

Disposable eye goggles with paper case. **$55-$75**

Zeiler red/green filter flashlight with Bakelite case. **$65-$85**

Winter relief token toy
K-98 rifle. **$20-$25**

Army gas mask, canister, and carrying strap.
$275-$325

Horsehair backpack for medic. **$250-$325**

Complementary mirror from uniform shop. **$125-$200**

K-98 rifle cleaning kit in storage tin box. **$85-$100**

Baltic cross vehicle id flag, grommets in corners,
3 ft. x 6 ft. **$375-$450**

Vehicle id flag with static swastika, grommets
in corners, 3 ft. x 6 ft. **$375-$450**

Soldbuch for well-decorated army soldier. **$175-$225**

Recruit training manual. **$45-$50**

Grouping for soldier with soldbuch, dogtag, wound badge, wound badge award document, triage tag, and miscellaneous letters. **$325-$400**

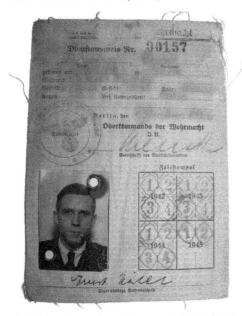

OKW headquarters id record. **$250-$275**

Army field series postcard. **$20-$25**

Army collector cigarette cards. **$15-$20**

Assault gun crewmember on his vehicle.

1940 soldier's calendar and propaganda book.
$45-$65

Assault gun crewmember's studio photo.

Decorations

Many decorations were distributed among the different branches of the armed forces, paramilitary, and civilian groups. Members of the Heer were the greatest recipients of these awards.

Paper packet to 2nd class war merit service cross without swords. **$25-$35**

Field award commendation for a close combat bar. **$75-$100**

Paper packet to 2nd class war merit service cross with swords. **$25-$35**

Issue paper packet for the 2nd class iron cross. **$35-$45**

Paper issue packet for Russian Front medal. **$35-$45**

Paper issue packet for the West Wall medal. **$25-$35**

Paper issue packet for third class wound badge. **$20-$25**

Award certificate for the second class war merit service cross with swords. **$45-$65**

German cross in gold for combatants. **$4500-$5000**
(JAG)

Second class silver wound badge,
solid back, in issue box. **$175-$225**

German cross in cloth and alloy. **$475-$575**

Third class black wound badge, solid back,
French maker. **$125-$150**

First class gold wound badge, solid back. **$250-$350**

Third class black wound badge,
hollow back. **$65-$75**

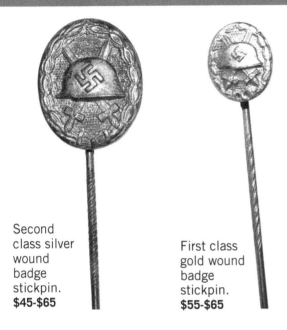

Second class silver wound badge stickpin. **$45-$65**

First class gold wound badge stickpin. **$55-$65**

Ribbon bar for Czechoslovakia entrance award with Prague bar. **$35-$45**

Second class silver close combat bar. **$450-$550**

Three-place medal bar with iron cross, war merit service cross, and Russian Front medals. **$225-$275**

Third class bronze close combat bar. **$275-$325**

Seven-place ribbon bar with iron cross, war merit service cross, and Russian Front medal. **$75-$95**

Three-place ribbon bar with iron cross, war merit service cross, and Russian Front medal ribbons. **$75-$85**

1st class iron cross in issue case. **$350-$475**

Convex 1st class iron cross in issue case. **$450-$550**

1st class iron cross variant, painted with brass center. **$275-$375**

2nd class iron cross. **$125-$145**

Variant 2nd class iron cross, painted with brass center. **$125-$145**

Second class iron cross lapel ribbon for civilian clothes. **$25-$25**

First class spang to the iron cross mounted above an Imperial 1st class iron cross. **$450-$600**

Unissued 2nd class iron cross with ribbon. **$175-$225**

Second class spang to the iron cross mounted on an Imperial 2nd class iron cross ribbon. **$275-$325**

First class war merit service cross. **$165-$225**

Second class war merit service cross lapel ribbon bar. **$35-$45**

Three-place war merit service cross, long service, and anschlus medals stickpin. **$65-$85**

Italian campaign medal. **$75-$95**

Unissued second class war merit service cross. **$75-$125**

Second class war merit service cross with swords. **$65-$85**

West Wall medal and ribbon. **$65-$85**

Czechoslovakia anschluss medal. **$85-$120**

Austrian anschluss medal.
$85-$120

Russian Front medal. **$65-$85**

Spanish Blue division Russian campaign medal. **$125-$145**

Bronze anti-partisan badge.
$750-$1,000

Romanian anti-Bolshevik medal.
$95-$135

Memel anschluss medal.
$150-$200

Narvik campaign shield.
$450-$575

Nine-place sew-on ribbon bar with army long service award and Imperial and Nazi ribbons. **$95-$125**

Ten-place ribbon bar with two army long service, Imperial, and Nazi awards. **$125-$145**

Winter relief porcelain army token pins: officer, panzer, and skiing soldiers. **$35-$50**

Winter relief metal bomb token pins. **$25-$30**

Tropical pith helmet insignias. **$100-$125**

Visor cap eagle. **$45-$65**

Visor cap wreath and roundel. **$45-$65**

National roundel for cap. **$15-$20**

Officer's summer white uniform breast eagle. **$125-$150**

Panzer collar death's-head insignia with prongs. **$40-$50**

Edelweiss for alpine corps cap. **$45-$55**

Panzer badge, pinback, maker-marked. **$325-$375**

Panzer shooting lanyard device. **$65-$85**

General assault badge. **$275-$325**

Assault gun badge in bronze. **$375-$425**

Second class silver driver's proficiency badge. **$55-$65**

First class gold driver's proficiency badge. **$75-$85**

Third class bronze driver's proficiency badge. **$45-$50**

Motorized troops infantry
assault badge. **$250-$300**

Army flak badge, early production
tombak. **$550-$700**

Infantry assault badge. **$175-$225**

Paper issue packet for infantry assault badge.
$35-$45

Plastic armed forces day tinnie. **$45-$65**

1939 day of the armed services tinnie. **$75-$95**

Armed services day tinnie. **$65-$85**

Army "train" (civilian retinue) workers stickpin. **$75-$95**

Calvary officer's watch fob with dedication. **$275-$350**

Gold driver's proficiency stickpin. **$45-$65**

Panzer badge stickpin. **$55-$75**

Luftwaffe

During World War I, the philosophy of combat changed from chivalrous contests between somewhat equal foes to murderous routes won by those who possessed the greater technical advantage. One of these newly introduced tools of warfare was the airplane, which started in the benign role of observation instrument but soon blossomed into a lethal weapon.

Through six years of conflict before its defeat, the German military recognized the value of a well-organized air force. When the Nazi Party came to power, they accelerated the clandestine buildup of military forces that had been suppressed by the Allied treaty. "Air sporting clubs" such as the DLV and the NSFK grew in the shadows by training future pilots and aircraft technicians. By 1935, Hitler openly publicized his plan for Germany's rearmament, setting great store in the enlargement of the German *Luftwaffe* (air force). Herman Goring, a World War I air ace, fanatical Nazi, and brutal minister of Hitler's Reich, was appointed commander-in-chief of this important military service.

Like many branches of the armed forces, the air corps was separated into multiple groups of specialists, such as flight personnel, maintenance, flak, paratroopers, ground troops, administration, and many others. The Luftwaffe was divided into *Luftflotten* (air fleets), which increased from four groups to seven as the war progressed. Each fleet was further divided into *Luftgaue* (air districts) and finally *Fliegerkorps* (air corps). Soldier ranks of service began with *Reichmarshall* (Herman Goering) through 11 officer ranks, eight NCO ranks, and five enlisted ranks, ending with *Flieger* (private).

Luftwaffe aircrews went through extensive training, ranging from 13 to 20 months with hundreds of flight time hours, depending on the types of aircraft and missions they were qualified to fly. The time dropped to 112 hours of flight training during the closing months of the war when the number of pilots rapidly decreased.

The first combat testing came in 1936 when Hitler formed the Condor Legion – made up of volunteers from the German air force and army – to help the Nationalists in the Spanish Civil War. The aircrews developed and mastered strategic bombing missions, dive-bombing, and aerial combat during the war, which lasted until Franco's final victory. When Poland was invaded in 1939, these skills were used to devastating effect, helping bring a quick victory to the German forces. By 1941, with the whole of Europe now involved in the world war, Germany's Luftwaffe ruled the skies. This changed rapidly when the United States became involved in the war, sending thousands of troops and aircraft into the European theatre.

The need for anti-aircraft artillery was first realized by the German military with the advent of unopposed raids by Allied planes during World War I. The first successful *Fliegerabwehrkanone* ("flak" is an acronym) units were developed by the *Kaiserliche Marine* (German naval service) in 1917. In the 1920s a clandestine program was carried out to equip and train flak operators.

Anti-aircraft weapons took many forms, from simple upturned machine gun installations to specifically designed cannons ranging in calibers from 12.7 to 128mm. The most successful were the 88mm cannons produced in four models – 18, 36, 37, and 41 – each with improvements in armor, carriage design, and shell velocity. As World War II progressed, the well-constructed 88mm units saw extensive use as anti-aircraft cannons and anti-tank pieces. In their anti-aircraft roles, timed charges designed to explode at designated heights spewed hot fragments in the hope of destroying or crippling enemy aircraft flying at high altitudes. Flak units were spread thickly, concentrated in belts up to 15 miles wide, around industrial complexes, military bases, or highly populated cities. Flak "towers," massive concrete structures built in urban areas, were designed to be impregnable to Allied bombings and serve as elevated flak positions and air raid shelters. Auxiliary units attached to flak positions wheeled large searchlights to illuminate Allied aircraft formations during night attacks. When Allied bombers flew over Axis-occupied countries, they feared the brutal pounding of German anti-aircraft guns. When seen approaching, enemy planes could be averted or fought, but searing shrapnel from flak came unannounced from the countryside below.

At its peak in 1942 there were over 15,000 88mm German anti-aircraft gun emplacements in the Third Reich, which made a major impact on the speed at which the Allies were able to advance their bombing strategies. But overall, flak anti-aircraft cannons had mixed results: Luftwaffe analysts estimated that it required an average of 3,300 88mm shells to shoot down an Allied aircraft. At the same time it was estimated that one Allied aircraft was destroyed by flak for every aircraft destroyed by fighter planes. On the ground, the flak cannon's agility and firepower felled many Russian, British, and American armored units.

All branches of the Luftwaffe wore basic three-quarter-length medium gray five-button wool (or finer fabrics for officers) service tunics with drop-down collars, four buttoned pockets, and matching pants or riding britches. Branch of service designation was signified by 13 different colors, such as golden yellow for flight and paratroopers, red for flak, and blue for medical; these were worn in the form of collar tabs and shoulder strap underlayment. Collar tabs featured a series of gull-shaped aluminum or embroidered pips, oak leaves, and piping that designated rank. Military awards, such as 1st class iron crosses, qualification badges, and ribbon bars were worn on the uniform in their respective places. During formal and parade occasions, full medal bars and aiguillettes replaced the more compact ribbon bars.

Brown leather belts were worn with cross straps until later in the war, with blue-painted, aluminum, or nickel silver buckles. Enlisted buckles were rectangular with an oval oak leaf wreath surrounding a flying eagle clutching a canted swastika. Officer's buckles were oval with the same oak leaf border but contained a gilded eagle and swastika affixed to the center. During full dress

occasions, officers would substitute a brocade belt for the leather model.

Uniforms were completed with gray overseas or visor caps and black boots or shoes. The enlisted overseas cap was usually made of coarse wool with a cloth flying eagle clutching a canted swastika over a roundel of the national colors mounted on the front. Officers' caps were of better-quality materials with silver piping around the cap fold edges and emblems of wire embroidery rather than plain cotton. Visor caps for enlisted and NCOs were made of gray wool with black mohair bands and black leather visors. The front of the caps bore a metal flying eagle clutching a canted swastika over a stylized oak leaf surround with two outstretched wings, in the center of which was a metal roundel in red and black surrounded by silver. A black leather chinstrap was secured across the upper leather brim of the visor with black buttons on either side of the hatband. Branch of service was again signified by the piping color around the upper border and cap band edges. Officers' caps were of the same basic design, but made of finer material with silver piping, or gold for general officers. Likewise, chinstraps were also silver or gold bullion, and cap devices were often made of higher-quality metal or bullion materials in silver or gold.

During formal occasions and when walking out, officers could carry either a *Fliegerdolch* (flyer's dagger) or *Fliegerschwert* (flyer's sword). The dagger, introduced in 1934, had a long double-edged blade with a winged silver crossguard containing an encircled gilt swastika, blue wire-wrapped spiral leather handle, and silver standing disk pommel with a gild rotated sun wheel swastika. The silver was eventually replaced with aluminum. The blade was mounted in a blue leather-bound scabbard with silver throat, bands and toe and an aluminum double-hanging chain. In 1937 the dagger was changed to a shorter double-edged model with an outstretched winged eagle crossguard clutching a rotated swastika. The celluloid spiral grip varied in color from white to dark orange and was wrapped with silver wire. The pommel cap was a stout oak leaf ball with a gilded swastika on either side. Daggers could be custom-ordered with engraved or Damascus blades at the time of purchase. The dagger handle was wrapped with a silver portepeed and rested in a pebbled silver scabbard with an oak leaf design on the toe, silver hanger suspension rings, and two-strap bullion gray hanger with oak leaf-embellished hooks and buckles. Enlisted men could not carry daggers but often sported dress bayonets with long or short (NCO) nickel-plated blades mounted in black diamond-patterned plastic or stag handles with nickel crossguards and bird's-head pommels. Black-painted scabbards were carried in brown leather or patent leather frogs with *troddels* (cloth straps and knots) attached to the upper sections.

The long Luftwaffe sword resembled the first model dagger, but with two suspension rings mounted across from one another on the scabbard throat, from which hung a blue leather hanger wrapped around the back of the scabbard, meeting at a third hanging loop. General officers carried an entirely different model of elaborate sword with a small thin blade, basket handguard, Luftwaffe eagle emblem, thin wire-wrapped handle, and flat oval pommel carried in a leather-wrapped gilt-toed and ringed scabbard.

Awards were given to Luftwaffe soldiers for acts of bravery or for completing requirements for specialized training. The *Flugzeugfuhrerabzeichen* (pilot's badge) was introduced in 1935 and awarded to each man who had earned his pilot's license. This award featured a multi-piece cutout silver oval oak leaf wreath with an eagle in profile with outstretched wings across the front and holding a large canted swastika. The *Beobachterabzeichen* (observer's badge) resembled the pilot's badge but had downswept wings and an open-topped wreath. This was awarded to crewmen who had completed five operation flights or two months of flight service. *Gemeinsames Flugzeugfuhrer Und Beobachterabzeichen* (combined pilot's and observer's badges) were similar in construction to the pilot's badge but the wreath was gilded. Flight personnel could also be awarded the *Fliegerschutzenabzeichen Fur Bordfunker* (radio operator/gunner badge), *Fliegerschutzenabzeichen Fur Bordschutzen Und Bordmechaniker* (air gunner/flight engineer badge), *Segelflugzeugfuhrerabzeichen* (glider pilot badge), as well as a series of flyers' clasps for fighters and bombers. Many of these awards were also produced in cloth versions (bullion thread for officers)

to be worn on everyday uniforms.

Several awards were unique to flak members, the first of which was the *Flak-Kampfabzeichen Der Luftwaffe* (anti-aircraft badge of the Luftwaffe). This was awarded following a series of combat actions (three downed aircraft or five unsuccessful attempts) or for a singular act of bravery. The nickel silver and later pot metal award consisted of an oval wreath surrounding an upturned cannon. On the upper edge was mounted an eagle in flight clutching a canted swastika. The reverse of this pinback award could have a maker's mark or be plain. The award was worn on tunics below the left breast pocket.

After a flak gunner, gun chief, or range finder completed nine months of service, he was awarded a cloth flak artillery specialist patch worn on the lower left sleeve of his tunic. Composed of gray and light gray thread or sometimes bullion, the patch featured a winged upturned cannon resting on oak leaves from the bottom of which a canted swastika was suspended.

Other branches of the Luftwaffe could earn awards specific to their groups, such as the *Erdk Ampfabzeichen Der Luftwaffe* (ground combat badge) for ground forces and the *Fallschirmschutzenabzeichen* (parachutist's badge) for paratroopers. All branches of the air service were eligible for iron crosses, wound badges, campaign medals or shields, and many other non-service specific

awards of the Third Reich. When in full dress, enlisted men and NCOs sometimes donned a Luftwaffe shooting lanyard, worn from the right shoulder board to the second tunic bottom. This blue and silver braided lanyard had a medal device at the top holding a silver oval wreath with flying eagle and swastika. Higher grades of Luftwaffe lanyards were designated by thin hanging cords with acorns or cannon shells on the tips.

Enlisted technical qualifications were displayed by sleeve insignia in woven gray and light gray silhouetted patches for various communication, mechanical, or other specialties.

When in the air, crews often wore leather flying jackets or jumpsuits and leather or cloth helmets with electronics and eye goggles. Small-caliber pistols (due to lack of cockpit room) and flare pistols were holstered on belts or carried in leg straps. Because so many German aircraft were shot down over the homeland toward the end of the war, flying personnel wore yellow armbands with an eagle/swastika and "Deutsche Luftwaffe" printed across the base. This prevented angry German mobs from killing their own downed flyers, mistaking them for Allied combatants responsible for the devastating bombing of their homeland.

As the war progressed, a more utilitarian cap (M-43) was developed and worn by members of the Luftwaffe. This cap resembled an overseas cap with earflaps and a soft bill.

Soldiers in flak stations or performing maintenance on aircraft often replaced their uniforms with less cumbersome and sturdier overalls. Identification discs in the standard Wehrmacht oval split dogtags contained a soldier's identity and unit information. Soldiers were expected to carry identification documents such as the Luftwaffe *soldbuch* (military pay book) and *fuhrerschein* (driver's license).

By late 1944, the German Luftwaffe had become a shadow of what it was five years earlier. Bombed airplane factories forced manufacturers into cramped underground facilities manned by inexperienced and often unwilling workers who could not produce the needed planes. Thousands of young pilots, led to believe they were doing the right thing for their country, were killed in the two-front war started by Hitler and his Nazi dictatorship. Dwindling numbers of flak units and ground troops were augmented with RAD members, men of other paramilitary and civilian groups, women, and Hitler Youth members. By the spring of 1945, the Allies flew virtually unopposed across the skies, crushing the German homeland and bringing the European war to an end.

Luftwaffe officer's quality visor cap with bullion insignia. **$775-$1,000**

Luftwaffe enlisted summer visor cap for flight personnel. **$1,100-$1,350**

Luftwaffe officer's visor cap, Erel Mfg. **$675-$950**

Luftwaffe enlisted visor cap for flight or paratrooper personnel. **$575-$800**

Luftwaffe female auxiliary overseas cap. **$450-$650**

Luftwaffe flak enlisted visor cap, unit-marked inside. **$475-$650**

Luftwaffe enlisted overseas cap. **$275-$375**

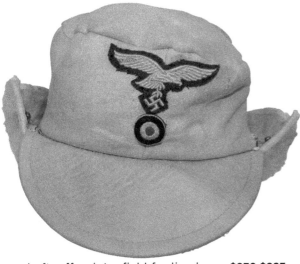

Luftwaffe winter field fur-lined cap. **$250-$325**

Luftwaffe leather flight helmet. **$275-$450**

Luftwaffe single decal helmet with liner and chinstrap. **$775-$900**

Luftwaffe field painted helmet, name and unit painted inside. **$450-$600**

Luftwaffe leather flight helmet with electronics. **$525-$650**

1918 transitional helmet with single decal and hand-painted unit shield. **$1,350-$2,000**

(Private Collection)

Enlisted flak tunic with ribbon bar, shooting lanyard, and flak badge. **$975-$1,150**

Flight NCO tunic with iron cross, shooting lanyard, wound badge, and cloth pilots badge, first model officer's dagger, belt, buckle, and enlisted visor cap. **$2,450-$3,575**
(Rick Fleury by JAG)

Medical officer tunic with ribbon bar, war merit service cross, and officer's cap. **$1,675-$1,950**

Child's flak tunic with toy bayonet, buckle and cross strap, ribbon bar, and wound badge. **$1,250-$1,500**

Leather "channel" flight jacket.
$900-$1,100
(Chris Depere)

Major bullion collar tabs for air ministry troops.
$200-$225
(Private Collection)

Flight captain bullion collar tabs. **$125-$150**

Captain's bullion collar tabs for signals troops.
$100-$125

(Private Collection)

Luftwaffe sports shirt. **$150-$195**

Flak Obergefreiter collar tab. **$35-$45**

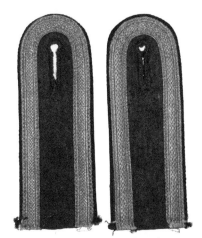

NCO shoulder boards for air ministry troops. **$85-$100**
(Private Collection)

Flight captain's braided shoulder boards. **$125-$150**

Flying division musician's wings. **$125-$175**

Tropical tunic collar insignia. **$65-$85**
(Private Collection)

NCO shoulder boards for signals troops. **$80-$100**
(Private Collection)

Flight NCO shoulder board. **$45-$60**

Supply and procurement service embroidered breast patch. **$95-$125**

Flak NCO shoulder board with litzen. **$35-$45**

Air control school NCO shoulder board. **$75-$85**

Air force construction personnel sleeve patch. **$95-$125**

Overalls sleeve rank insignia. **$25-$40**
(Private Collection)

Bullion officer visor cap eagle and wreath.
$150-$175
(Private Collection)

Large Luftwaffe sports vest eagle. **$85-$100**

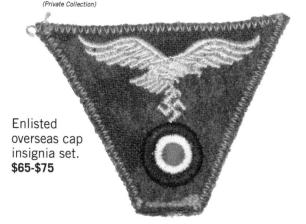

Enlisted overseas cap insignia set.
$65-$75

Luftwaffe paratrooper smock eagle. **$85-$100**

Enlisted tunic breast eagle.
$65-$85

Enlisted rank chevron. **$25-$35**

Tropical enlisted tunic breast eagle.
$125-$175
(Private Collection)

Flying technical specialty patch.
$45-$65

Small Luftwaffe sports vest eagle.
$65-$75

Flying personnel specialty patch.
$45-$55

Rangefinder specialty arm patch. **$35-$45**

Sound location specialty patch. **$25-$35**

Radio operator specialty patch. **$25-$35**

Directional radio operator specialty patch. **$25-$35**

Aircraft warning specialty patch. **$25-$35**

Signals equipment specialty patch. **$25-$35**

Telephone operator specialty patch. **$25-$35**

Medical specialty patch. **$35-$45**

Transport driver specialty patch with gold braid. **$45-$65**

Air radio operator/gunner cloth badge. **$125-$150**

Small arms ordinance specialty patch. **$25-$35**

Ordinance technician specialist patch. **$25-$35**

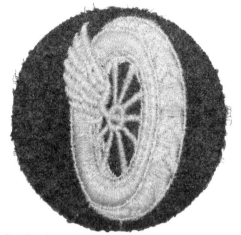

Mechanized transport specialist patch. **$45-$65**

Signals specialty patch. **$25-$35**

Flak personnel specialty award. **$65-$85**

Flying personnel armband. **$350-$450**

Officer's early drop-tail eagle buckle and brocade dress belt. **$450-$675**

Luftwaffe enlisted belt buckle and fob, blue paint. **$175-$225**

Enlisted aluminum belt buckle on patent leather parade belt. **$325-$375**

Luftwaffe enlisted belt buckle, aluminum. **$150-$175**

Luftwaffe nickel officer's sword with teardrop hanger. **$1,250-$1,500**

Luftwaffe aluminum officer's sword with teardrop hanger. **$1,150-$1,400**

Luftwaffe paratrooper or flight crew gravity knife, initials carved in handle. **$450-$650**

Second model Luftwaffe officer's dagger with double engraved blade. **$1,650-$2,600**

Second model Luftwaffe officer's dagger, no maker's mark, later finish. **$525-$675**

First model Luftwaffe officer's dagger with chain hanger. **$675-$800**

Luftwaffe mess hall spoons. **$45-$75**

Luftwaffe issue-marked boot knife. **$275-$350**

Luftwaffe field recovered ripcord handles. **$85-$100**

1941 Luftwaffe paratrooper training school souvenir plate. **$250-$300**

Winter relief plastic bi-wing plane. **$35-$45**

Flak man's dogtags. **$75-$100**

Wooden Luftwaffe school chair, marked on underside. **$375-$500**

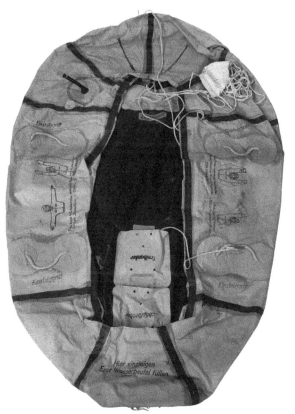

Flight personal flotation raft, instruction-marked. **$475-$650**

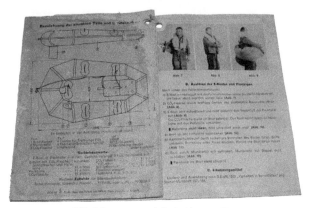

Flight personal flotation raft instruction booklet. **$50-$75**

Luftwaffe flak officer's driver's license. **$75-$95**

Luftwaffe soldbuch. **$100-$150**

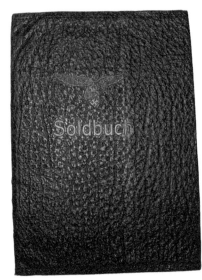

Leatherette private-purchase cover for Luftwaffe soldbuch. **$75-$95**

Luftwaffe vehicle driver's license. **$75-$95**

Luftwaffe paratrooper photo album. **$375-$500**

Luftwaffe helferin standing with two SA Feldherrnhalle guards.

Leatherette flying document wallet. **$75-$100**

Autographed Herman Goering postcard with an inscription on the back by the GI who received it from Goring at the Nuremburg prison. **$850-$1,000**

Studio photos of Luftwaffe NCO in service and flight uniforms.

Herman Goring table medal award for technical service to the Luftwaffe. **$350-$450**

Nine-place ribbon bar with Imperial, Nazi, and two Luftwaffe long service awards. **$125-$150**

Eight-place ribbon bar with Nazi political and combat ribbons and two Luftwaffe long service awards. **$135-$165**

Nine-place medal bar with Imperial, Nazi, and Luftwaffe long service awards. **$600-$800**

Seven-place civilian mount medal bar with Spanish, Nazi, and Luftwaffe long service awards. **$650-$850**

Luftwaffe long service medal on parade mount. **$125-$150**

Luftwaffe visor cap eagle with prongs. **$45-$65**

Luftwaffe officer's summer tunic pinback breast eagle. **$150-$200**

Luftwaffe tropical pith helmet devices. **$250-$275**

Luftwaffe supply and procurement service breast eagle. **$150-$195**

Luftwaffe visor cap wreath and roundel with prongs. **$45-$65**

Doorman visor cap insignia with prongs. **$100-$135**

Civilian air sea rescue visor cap badge. **$350-$425**

Combination pilot's/observer's badge in case.
$875-$1,100
(JAG)

Luftwaffe paratrooper badge. **$450-$675**

Luftwaffe pilot's pinback badge. **$475-$650**

Luftwaffe ground assault pinback badge. **$375-$475**

Luftwaffe flak pinback badge. **$295-$375**

Winter relief porcelain flight and officers donation pins. **$45-$55**

Air gunner/ flight engineer pinback badge. **$500-$650**
(Private Collection)

Luftwaffe female auxiliary membership pin. **$195-$250**

Imperial pilot's badge often worn by older Nazi officers. **$750-$1,100**
(Private Collection)

Krim campaign shield with gray Luftwaffe backing. **$375-$450**

Civilian retinue pin in zinc. **$65-$75**

Civilian retinue pin in bronze. **$75-$90**

Plastic Luftwaffe flying troops donation pin. **$45-$55**

Plastic Luftwaffe smoke troops donation pin. **$35-$45**

Plastic Luftwaffe flak troops donation pin. **$35-$45**

Civilian retinue stickpin in aluminum. **$75-$90**

Luftwaffe supply and procurement stickpin for civilian clothing. **$125-$150**

Luftwaffe service stickpin to wear with civilian clothing. **$85-$125**

Kriegsmarine

At first a minor segment of the German armed forces from the early 18th century, the German navy did not become a significant part of the country's overall fighting force until the later part of the 19th century. Under the unified Imperial states forming the new Germany, naval ships became larger and battle plans more far-reaching, changing from coastal defense to seaworthy attack forces.

The naval forces saw exponential growth under Kaiser Wilhelm II as he readied the nation for the aggressive battles that were to become World War I. After the war ended, the German navy was virtually dissolved, shrunk to a force of 15,000 soldiers with just a few capital ships and smaller vessels at their disposal.

Later, Adolf Hitler began an aggressive program of rearmament, taking the downsized navy to greater heights than those of the kaiser. State-of-the-art battleships, cruisers, and, above all, a fleet of deadly submarines were built, and thousands of new recruits trained for his vision of future conquests. By 1939, the German navy was one of the most advanced and sophisticated military bodies on the high seas.

The Kriegsmarine was divided into four primary branches: *Uberwasserstrietkrafte* (surface ships) comprised of all battleships, cruisers, and other surface ships; *U-Boote* (submarine service); *Marine Artillerie* (coastal artillery); and *Marinebeamten* (naval administration) consisting of office, professional, and other administrative personnel. The navy also incorporated the *Luftwaffenkommando See* (Naval Air Force Command – not a naval branch, but part of the Luftwaffe) for rescue services, surveillance, and air attacks.

Ranking within the Kriegsmarine consisted of 14 officers' ranks, beginning with *Fahnrich zur See* to *Grossadmiral;* six non-commissioned officers' ranks (*Maat* to *Stabsoberbootsmann*); and six enlisted ranks (*Matrose* to *Matrosen-Stabsobergefreiter*).

Basic uniforms for enlisted men consisted of dark blue heavy cloth jumpers worn with wide, drop-down rear collars with three white stripes around the perimeters and matching blue bellbottom pants. A yellow national eagle over wreath and swastika was sewn to the right breast of the blouse. A black leather belt with gilded or blue-gray finished rectangular buckle with a half oak leaf wreath, supporting the arched motto *"Gott Mit Uns"* surrounding an eagle perched on a canted swastika, finished the outfit.

Summer uniforms were made of lighter-weight white fabric with broad, dark blue stripes on the shirt cuffs and a dark blue eagle on the breast. A blue double-breasted dress jacket with two rows of gilded buttons, five buttons on each cuff along with ranking stripes, and a yellow or gilded-thread breast eagle was worn for formal occasions or when "walking out." Military (or some paramilitary, if authorized) awards were worn on their respective places on the tunic front. Chevrons and sleeve patches designated rank and job specialty, such as signal or torpedo man.

During inclement weather, a sailor wore a heavy dark blue wool peacoat with cornflower blue and bullion striped ranking collar patches, ratings, and specialty patches on the sleeves. Black leather shoes and a dark blue *Matrosenmutze* – traditional brimless Donald Duck-style sailor cap – with the ship's name or station emblazoned across the front of the cap tally (band) were worn. For security reasons, this practice was later changed to only the word "Kriegsmarine" on the tally. Above the tally was a gilded metal eagle with wreath and swastika over a roundel with the national colors. A white cover could be worn on the upper portion of the cap when the sailor was stationed in tropical areas. In 1938 a *Bordmutze* (overseas cap) similar in design to caps worn by the other military branches was introduced in dark blue fabric with yellow eagle, wreath, and swastika over a national roundel. A white version was later produced for wear in tropical areas.

Officers wore a traditional dark blue double-breasted naval tunic with two rows of gilded anchor buttons. Rank was shown by the addition of a series of gold bullion stripes on the lower sleeves and various cloth and gold wire shoulder boards, when used. Tunics sported gold bullion eagles, wreaths, and swastikas on the right breasts, with awards worn in their respective places on the tunic's front. Matching pants, black shoes, white shirt, and black tie completed the uniform.

Summer versions of the standard uniform consisted of lighter fabric white tunics and trousers. The sewn version of the national breast eagle was replaced with a gilded metal piece that was pinned to the right tunic front.

In cold weather, officers wore a long, heavy blue woolen double-breasted service coat, sometimes finished with black fabric (or bullion for dress occasions) belt and buckle. The buckle contained a gilded oval oak leaf pattern surrounding a fouled naval anchor.

Caps were either visor-style or overseas models. The visor cap was made of fine quality dark blue woolen material with a wide black-ribbed cap band. A tall embroidered gilded oak leaf wreath surrounding a national roundel was mounted on the front of the band with a national eagle, wreath, and swastika sewn above. Rank was further designated by the addition of a row of scalloped or oak leaf decorations around the visor border. A black leather chinstrap with buckle supported by gilded buttons rested on the visor base. Officers could place removable white covers on their caps during the summer months.

If stationed in tropical areas, officers and enlisted men often wore light tan-colored, four-pocket canvas uniforms with gold buttons, yellow breast eagles, and

dark blue sleeve and collar ratings. Administrative officers wore the same blue uniforms as combat officers except their insignias were silver rather than gold. In addition, administrative visor caps had no decorations on the visors.

For formal occasions, officers could wear a beautiful naval dagger or naval sword. The 1938 model Kriegsmarine dagger consisted of a long double-edged blade, often etched or engraved with floral and marine designs. The rounded handle was of white celluloid-covered wood or ivory with a spiral wire wrap. The crossguard was straight with rounded tips with a fouled anchor in the center and a button catch on the backside. The pommel cap featured a golden eagle with folded wings standing on a wreath-enclosed swastika. The dagger was housed in a gilded scabbard with "lightning bolt" or "hammered" designs hung from two suspension rings. The attaching hanger was made of two pieces: black cloth sewn stripes with golden lion's-head buckles, swivels and chain. A silver portepeed was elaborately wound around the upper and lower sections of the handle and crossguards. Administrative officers could also wear daggers, but with silver instead of gilded metal parts.

The marine sword had a long polished or plated blade with a gilded "D" guard, back strap and lion's-head pommel, with or without red and green faceted glass eyes, mounted over a white celluloid and wire-bound grip. The clamshell crossguard contained a fouled anchor and was hinged to allow the owner to fold the guard up for storage and variant wear. The scabbard of black leather had a gilded metal drag, throat, and center band, the last two bearing suspension rings. Hangers were black leather with lion's-head buckles in gilded metal, and long golden portepeeds were tied to the lower "D" guards.

Land forces, such as coastal artillery sailors, wore dark gray tunics and pants similar to army uniforms. However, tunic buttons were gold with a fouled anchor design, eagles were yellow gold, and collar and shoulder board braiding (if applicable) were gold rather than silver litzen. These sailors wore gray overseas caps with gold eagles and national roundels, or regulation Wehrmacht helmets with gray-green paint and gold eagle and swastika side shields.

Officers and men of the Kriegsmarine earned war badges based on service requirements and training. These included the *U-Boot Kriegsabzeichen* (submariner's war badge), the *Flotten Kriegsabzeichen* (high seas war badge), or the *Kriegsabzeichen Fur Die Marineartillerie* (coastal artillery badge), among others. They were worn in their respective places on the tunic, along with non-specific branch awards like an iron cross. Medal bars were worn during parades and formal occasions, replaced by ribbon bars during everyday wear.

Other specialty uniforms were worn as required by the type of work performed by the sailors. Overalls, leather foul weather suits, and other outfits were commonplace aboard ships and on land installations. Members of the submarine corps were famous for the variations of civilian and military outfits they wore during their long and arduous patrols at sea.

Women auxiliaries were employed in many naval installations as secretaries, cooks, and other non-combatant roles. A typical auxiliary uniform consisted of a dark blue blazer with yellow collar piping, blue skirt, white blouse, and black leather shoes. The

tunic had a cuff title with the word *Marinehelferin* embroidered in yellow thread across the face. A blue overseas cap with yellow piping featured an eagle over swastika stitched high on the cap front with no roundel below.

Because many sailors and officers of the Kriegsmarine were not physically involved in the day-to-day political and social controls exercised in the Third Reich, and because of the navy's history of having more conservative, free-thinking members, fanatical Nazis were rarer in the naval ranks than in other land-based services. Even so, sailors followed their orders as directed by Hitler's command, dying by the thousands on and under the seas. More than 700 U-boats alone were destroyed during the war, taking with them 30,000 crewmembers. Only as the fighting came to a close did many captains allow their ships to break ranks and surrender to the Allies they felt would give them the best treatment.

Donald Duck first-style enlisted sailor's cap. **$950-$1,100**
(JAG)

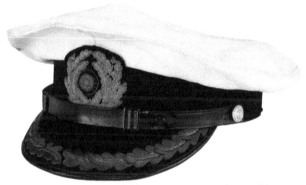

Officer's summer-topped visor cap with bullion insignia. **$2,400-$3,300**
(JAG)

Female auxiliary's overseas cap. **$400-$525**

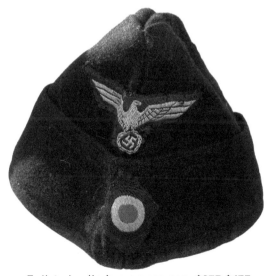

Enlisted sailor's overseas cap. **$375-$475**

Naval foul weather leather jacket with cruiser collar and eagle M stamped on breast. **$750-$900**

Naval officer's reefer jacket with ribbon bar, high seas badge, and iron cross ribbon in buttonhole, named in the pocket. **$1,100-$1,400**

Enlisted seaman's summer white jumper. **$400-$550**

Leather pants for naval foul weather jacket. **$175-$250**

Kriegsmarine cap tally for enlisted sailors, uncut. **$85-$125**

Musicians specialty patch. **$25-$35**

Enlisted sailor's summer white bellbottom pants. **$175-$200**

Seaman's patch. **$25-$35**

Minelayer specialty patch. **$25-$35**

Radio operator specialty patch. **$25-$35**

Medical specialty patch. **$25-$35**

Marine artillery specialty patch. **$25-$35**

Signals petty officer patch. **$35-$45**

Electrician specialty patch. **$25-$35**

Petty officer metal and cloth patch. **$50-$65**

Senior anti-aircraft gunner specialty patch. **$25-$35**

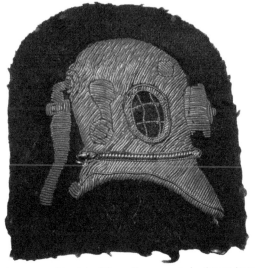

Early or pre-Nazi bullion divers patch. **$475-$600**

Enlisted uniform breast eagle. **$50-$65**

Kriegsmarine sports vest eagle. **$75-$95**

Kriegsmarine officer's dagger, double engraved blade, lightning bolt scabbard with two-piece hangers and portepeed. **$1,250-$1,650**

Kriegsmarine officer's dress lion's-head sword with issuance mark and undercoat carrying hanger/belt. **$1,200-$1,450**

Kriegsmarine officer's dagger, double engraved blade, hammered scabbard. **$975-$1,200**

German sailor's studio portrait. **$5-$15**

Naval war flag, marked on bunting edge, 6 ft. x 10 ft. **$475-$650**

Kriegsmarine female auxiliary in uniform. **$10-$15**
(Private Collection)

Sailors in heavy weather gear. **$5-$12**

Soldbuch for KIA enlisted sailor wearing a winter peacoat and jumper in the photograph. **$125-$175**

Soldbuch for an officer in tropical uniform. **$150-$175**

Merchant marine identification and record book, well-filled. **$175-$200**

Nazi Party Day souvenir book property-stamped to a Kriegsmarine naval base. **$65-$85**

Ribbon bar with long service awards. **$45-$55**

Eagle and cockade from an enlisted sailor's Donald Duck-style cap. **$75-$85**

Officer's summer tunic pinback breast eagle. **$150-$185**

Female auxiliary uniform throat brooch. **$200-$250**
(Private Collection)

Auxiliary Cruiser war badge, pinback. **$450-$575**

Female auxiliary uniform throat brooch variant. **$150-$200**
(Private Collection)

High seas fleet war badge, pinback. **$450-$600**

Destroyer war badge, pinback,
maker-marked. **$450-$575**

Blockade Runner's war badge, pinback. **$450-$575**

Minesweeper's war badge, pinback. **$275-$350**

Winter relief
donation porcelain
sailor pin. **$45-$55**

Submariner's war badge, pinback,
unmarked plated zinc. **$450-$575**

Plastic Kriegsmarine flag donation pin. **$35-$45**

Deutsche Reichsbahn (DR)

When Adolf Hitler led the German nation into the conflicts of World War II, the logistics of transporting war materials within and outside the Reich became the lifeblood of the war's progression.

Although Hitler spent large amounts of money and manpower to develop roadways across the country, railroads were by far the largest carriers of materials during the six years of war. Weapons, vehicles, provisions, and troops were carried by rail into the fray as the German army, air force, navy, and Waffen SS destroyed their foes in the early years of the war. As countries were conquered, trains began to carry more ominous cargo. Killing teams rounded up Jews, gypsies, and others deemed undesirable by the Nazi hierarchy and shipped them to work or death camps.

The German railroad began as a horse-drawn rail system in the 1830s and progressed to steam power within a few years. Before the nation's unification in 1871, the various German state monarchies fostered development of rail systems either owned by industrialists, the states themselves, or larger municipalities.

During World War I, the railroad played its first major military role as it carried troops and supplies across the country to the war front. After Germany's defeat, Allied reparations decimated their equipment, but the railroads persevered and grew. In 1920, the various *Landerbahnen* (small state railroads) were united to form the *Reichsbahn* (national state railroad). In 1939, the Reichsbahn – a civilian organization – carried covert German troops to the Polish border, beginning the European armed conflicts of World War II.

The railroad systems were 79% owned by the Reichsbahn and 21% privately owned. Trams or streetcars, another form of railed traffic, were commonly owned by the municipalities they served or by private companies for profit.

During the Third Reich, the service uniforms of railroad employees remained mostly the same as those worn during the Weimar period of the 1920s. Dark blue coats were worn with black slacks, white shirts, black ties (if open-collared), and black shoes or boots. Personnel could wear their civilian and military awards, such as party awards or iron crosses, affixed to the front of their tunics in their respective places. While performing the dirtier jobs of working on rolling stock or other heavy machinery, workers often wore coarse-woven, plain-colored two-piece work suits or coveralls.

Though the basic uniforms remained unchanged, the insignias were altered dramatically during Hitler's regime. Being a civilian group, the rail system did not use military ranks. Instead it divided employees into four main working classifications with 23 pay grades, varying from *Anwarter* to *Direktor*. These were designated by a series of collar patches, shoulder boards, and cuff titles beginning in 1936. In 1941, the Reichsbahn – under its parent organization, the SS – saw insignias further changed by the additions of bright gold swastika, oak leaves, and cords for advanced leaders to the winged wheel of the collar tabs, along with updated shoulder boards. In addition, breast eagles of gold thread on a black background and shoulder eagles with area names were added to some uniforms. As the war progressed, shoulder boards were further changed to the "passant" style, shortened and rotated 90 degrees, similar to those worn on modern U.S. Army officers' dress coats.

A peaked cap of dark blue wool featured red piping and a black mohair band fronting a cap badge of a winged wheel around a national cockade under an eagle, oak leaf wreath, and canted swastika. The cap's chinstrap, in various blue and gold colors, also signified rank. Overseas caps often used in everyday wear were also dark blue and red-piped with a sewn or metal national cap device. Conductors wore a bright red peaked cap, making them more visible in crowds in and around the train cars.

When in non-descript-style clothing, personnel could wear armbands designating their affiliations, which varied in color and script but usually took the form of a plain yellow or green background with the black lettering, "Deutsche Reichsbahn." When not in uniform, railroad employees could display their trade by proudly wearing stickpins or pinback insignias featuring a winged wheel.

Women Reichsbahn auxiliaries worked in traditional clerical roles before the war but took more active positions, such as conductors, as men were sent into combat. Women's uniforms were similar in appearance to their male counterparts with black skirts substituting the men's black pants. Because of rapid changes, many members never received uniform upgrades, resulting in a variety of old and new styles worn until the end of the war.

A special division of the Reichsbahn was the *Bahschutzpolizei* (state railroad protection police). These individuals, under direct command of the SS, were charged with protecting the property of the railroad and preventing and investigating crimes on raid vehicles and land.

Police uniforms consisted of light blue-gray tunics and trousers, belts, boots or shoes, and matching peaked caps with stylized oak leaf wreaths surrounding a national cockade under an eagle, oak leaf wreath, and canted swastika. Belts were black leather with rectangular silver buckles for lower ranks or round buckles for senior ranks. The buckles featured a winged railroad wheel overlaid by a canted swastika with the words "Deutsche Reichsbahn" in the surrounding circle.

At the outbreak of war, officers were typically armed with pistols carried in flap-over holsters, rifles, or machine guns.

During dress occasions, Bahnschutz officers and senior railroad officials could wear an authorized dagger, which came in two variations. The first model, in 1935, was similar to the standard Third Reich army dagger with a two-sided polished blade, oak leaf and acorn-embellished ferule and pommel cap, roll tipped crossguard with eagle over a round oak leaf wreath surrounding a canted swastika, and celluloid spiraled handle. The main difference between the railroad dagger and the army dagger was that that handle was cast in black to dark purple rather than white to orange plastic. The dagger was mounted in a pebbled silver-tone scabbard with two suspensions rings.

A second model dagger was introduced in 1938. The crossguard was changed from the eagle motif to a winged rail wheel, the pommel cap was redesigned into a domed shape, and ornamentation was added to the scabbard tow. Both versions were worn suspended from a silver and black striped two-strap hanger with silver clips and buckles.

Though a specific Reichsbahn sword was never developed, senior ranks were authorized to wear military-styled standard or lion's-head swords during formal occasions. Standard swords consisted of plain "D" guard NCO-type pieces with unembellished one-piece smooth backstraps and pommels over plain crossguards. These were produced in silver or gilded metal around a black celluloid wire-wound grip. A lion's-head version was authorized in gilded metal with green glass jeweled eyes. The sword officially accepted for use by the Reichsbahn had a winged wheel stamped into the underside of the crossguard. Swords could be adorned with a portepeed of dark blue and a silver strap from which was suspended a black and silver acorn.

As the war progressed, the Reichsbahn incorporated scores of rail lines in the conquered territories. By 1942, Slavs, Ukrainians, Russians, and many others became willing and unwilling members of the 1.4 million Reichsbahn force operating thousands of engines and cars over 50,000 miles of tracks. Ongoing partisan activities and the intensified bombing missions of the Allied air corps eventually devastated the German rail system, killing many of its workers. As more and more bridges and rail yards were destroyed, German armed forces and civilians alike were literally starved into submission, aiding the eventual defeat of Adolf Hitler and the Nazi regime.

Reichsbahn porter's visor cap. **$650-$775**

Reichsbahn visor cap. **$275-$450**

Weimar upgraded Nazi tram driver's tunic. **$450-$650**

Reichsbahn collar tab. **$75-$100**

Reichsbahn worker's armband. **$135-$175**

Reichsbahn shoulder shields with regional names. **$85-$125**

Reichsbahn police belt and buckle. **$425-$575**

Reichsbahn, Korbach sports certificate stamp. **$110-$150**

Winter relief porcelain donation pin, railroad worker. **$35-$45**

Uncut strip of six Reichsbahn breast eagles. **$175-$250**

Reichsbahn baggage claim ticket and tag. **$35-$45**

Ausweis for a Reichsbahn worker. **$75-$95**

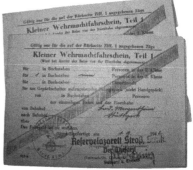

Reichsbahn short trip tickets for military personnel. **$25-$35**

Reichsbahn traveler's map and train route book. **$50-$75**

Streetcar visor cap insignia with prongs. **$150-$185**

Nationalsozialistische Frauenschaft (NSF)

Deutsches Frauenwerk (DFW)

During the era of Imperial Germany, many civic organizations contained female auxiliary sections that allowed women to participate in these male-dominated groups and helped the organizations operate efficiently by performing traditional female roles.

After the German defeat of World War I, the chaotic political and social scenery raised some of these conventional support positions to new heights of activity and responsibility. Nowhere was this more evident than the women who fell under the spell of Adolf Hitler and the fledgling Nazi party.

Though the basic philosophy of the Nazi party was that women served the country best as non-politically inclined wives and mothers, the early party found no issue with allowing females into the membership ranks.

Beginning in 1921, women became actively involved with the early meetings of the NSDAP and its charismatic new speaker, Adolf Hitler. When volunteering for service to the party, most women continued with the customary roles of performing clerical activities and helping the sick and injured from street and meeting brawls. However, more ardent female followers left these duties behind to make speeches, distribute propaganda flyers, and even take part in street fighting with Communists and other enemies of National Socialism.

Sundry small groups of women had loosely gathered from the start, but in 1923, one group, the *Deutscher Frauenorden* (German women's order) was formally organized by Elsbeth Zander as a part of the Nazi party. This and other residual groups of approximately 20,000 members, including the *Arbeitsgemienschaft voelkisch gesinnter Frauen* (Association of Racialist Women) and the *Rotes Hakenkreuz* (red swastika), were combined in 1931 by Adolf Hitler to form the *Nationalsozialistische Frauenschaft* (NSF). In 1934, Gertrude Scholz-Klink became the head of the NSF, a position she held until the end of World War II. The requirements for joining

the NSF were that the candidate be a minimum of 21 years of age, be able to demonstrate her racial purity, and be a strong advocate for the principles of the Nazi cause. Due to the fear of having too many unqualified members, entry into the NSF was closed to the general population – with some exceptions for long-term BDM party members or others deemed desirable – in 1936.

In 1934 the *Deutsches Frauenwerk* (DFW, German Women's Work) began. This organization was comprised of women who were more politically neutral than those in the NSF but still could be used and controlled by the central Nazi party. The group's general function was to assist with farming, nursing, domestic jobs, and activities for men and women who had devoted their time to the future war industry. Scholz-Klink became the leader of the DFW as well as the organized female sections of the *Deutsche Arbeitsfront* (DAF, Labor Corps), *Deutsches Rotes Kreuz* (DRK, German Red Cross), and many other social welfare organizations with over 20 million members under her control by the beginning of the war.

Ranking levels within the NSF began with the *Reichsfrauenfueherin* (Scholz-Klink), followed by 40 *Gaufrauenschaftsfuehrerinne* (district heads), 800 *Kreisfrauenschaftsfueherinnin* (county heads), and 28,000 *Ortsfrauenschaftsfueherinnen* (local leaders). There were about 3,000 paid professional leaders in the organization with the balance being volunteers. Professional staff members were trained in one of two Reich's level schools, while selected volunteers attended one of the 41 Gau level schools. The young attendees were trained for the positions they were to hold in the organization, learning the basics of National Socialist accepted principles of self-sacrifice for the state, marriage, maternity care, child-rearing, music, physical fitness, social graces, and anti-religious views. Home economics, the use of German-only manufactured goods, and advanced agricultural lessons were taught, making the members feel more self-sufficient in the new Germany. In addition, racial superiority and Nazi political doctrine were the main focus of the school training, which was carried back to and shared within the local levels of the NSF. Members passed these ideas and new technical skills to their families and other members of their communities to promote the social good and belief in the party.

During the war, NSF members helped German servicemen by providing refreshments to troops in transit, the police by helping to distribute food in times of shortage in market areas, and to work as guardians for young women employed on military bases. NSF women worked with many other sanctioned civilian, paramilitary, and military groups, providing a conduit for incoming information, outgoing propaganda, and control by the centralized Nazi state. By the beginning of the war, the NSF had over 2.3 million active members.

Uniforms were worn by the career women of the NSF but not by most volunteers. Though regulations were somewhat lax for volunteers, basic uniforms for career members consisted of dark blue jackets and skirts worn with white broad-collared blouses. The jackets included a bullion eagle clasping a round wreath of oak leaves containing a canted swastika sewn to the left upper arm and an embroidered group cuff title on the left sleeve. Black shoes and a white or dark broad-brimmed hat with a silk ribbon were used during formal occasions. If not wearing civilian clothing, volunteers wore white blouses and dark skirts or gray jumpers with their membership insignia. The most identifying symbol of the NSF was the *Abzeichen fur Mitglieder der N.S. Frauenschaft* (badge of the Nazi Women's League) worn on the left breast of uniforms or civilian clothing.

The first of three types of NSF membership pins resembled the regular NSDAP enamel membership badge: 23.5mm red circle surrounding a white center with a black canted swastika in the center. Instead of the NSDAP script surrounding the white center, the words *"Fraueneschaft-NSDAP"* were substituted in silver lettering. This type was only used in 1933.

In 1934 the second basic type triangular badge appeared, 27mm high by 25.5mm wide with a white enamel cross in the center over a black enamel background. A white enamel border across the top contained the words *"Nat Soz Frauenschaft"* with a static red swastika in the center of the cross. On each cross arm and at the cross base were the letters G, H, and L, which stood for *Glaube, Hoffnung, Liebe* (faith, hope, and love). Leadership ranks were also shown by the addition of colored enameled outer borders: blue for *Orts* (local), black and later white for *Kreis* (county), red for *Gau* (region), and yellow for *Reich* (country). These badges were produced in small and large versions to be

purchased and worn at each woman's discretion.

In 1939 the final series NFS badge was issued. It no longer contained a cross in the center, instead featuring either a rounded sun wheel swastika for basic members or a silver eagle with wreath and swastika for upper levels, positioned above a silver German life rune over a black enamel background. The top silver bar bore the words *"N.S. Frauenschaft."* This third type of badge still incorporated the colored borders for level, but also added silver oak leaf borders for leader levels.

The first type badge had *ges gesch* (patent pending) and the manufacturer's name on the reverse, while the second and third types had RZM codes and "M" manufacturers' code numbers.

Variations in these badges were produced for non-members of the NSF, such as the *Andere Kolleginnen der NS Frauenschaft* (non-member support personnel) and *Ehemaliganabzeichen der N.S. Frauenschaft* (badge for ex-NSF members), among others. As the war depleted supplies and manpower, NSF badges were produced in painted zinc rather than enamel.

An oversized cloth emblem resembling the NSF badge was worn on working or sporting clothes to show affiliation with the group. Each NSF member carried an *NS Frauenschaft Mitgliedsbuch* (membership book) with name, birthday, occupation, address, and other personal information written in the front, with places in the rear for monthly dues stamps. These could be carried in leatherette custom-purchased covers by more affluent members.

When attending meetings or congregating for community service, NSF groups frequently hung beautifully made printed metal or fabric banners at their localities to signify their presence and direct members to the leadership locations. Many of the elaborately embroidered banners were custom-made by members of the local groups.

The 800,000 members of the *Deutsches Frauenwerk* (DFW) did not wear uniforms. They wore the normal attire of their trade, such as nursing uniforms, with the addition of their own distinct membership pins or patches. The *Abzeichen des Deutschen Frauenwerkes* (badge of German Women's Work) was similar to the basic third type NSF badge with the words *"Deutsches Frauenwerk"* written in red script across the upper border. An oversized black and white cloth emblem, similar to the badge, was worn on blouse sleeves and sports vests to signify membership in the group.

When Hitler and the NSDAP came to power, all non-

Nazi-affiliated women's groups were quickly engulfed by the party and phased out of existence. By the war's end, the Allies recognized the danger of allowing the fervent Nazi membership of the NSF to continue to spread their hatred and resistance to Germany's future democracy, and so rapidly disbanded the women's flag bearer of the Third Reich.

Frauenschaft uncut sleeve patch. **$75-$95**

Frauenschaft uncut sleeve or sports vest cloth patch. **$75-$95**

Frauenschaft membership and dues booklet. **$125-$150**

Frauenschaft/Frauenwerk uncut sleeve patch. **$150-$175**

Private-purchase leatherette cover for Frauenschaft membership booklet. **$225-$275**

Yearbook for the Frauenschaft. **$85-$135**

Frauenschaft local group Bracht handmade two-sided standard, gold rope fringe, 3 ft. x 3-1/2 ft. **$750-$1,000**

Frauenschaft dedication banner. **$75-$125**

Table medal, 3rd place art award for women. **$225-$325**

Frauenschaft type 2 staff member's enamel badge, Kreis level, RZM-marked on reverse. **$175-$225**

Frauenschaft type 2 enamel membership badge, Orts level, pinback, RZM-marked on reverse. **$125-$150**

Frauenschaft type 2 leader's enamel membership badge, Gau level, pinback, RZM-marked on reverse. **$275-$350**

Frauenschaft type 3 staff enamel badge, Orts level, pinback, RZM-marked on reverse. **$225-$275**

Frauenschaft type 3 staff painted badge, Orts level, pinback, RZM-marked on reverse. **$200-$250**

Frauenschaft type 3 leader's membership badge, Orts level, pinback, RZM-marked on reverse. **$250-$275**

Frauenschaft type 3 staff enamel badge, Reich's level, pinback, RZM-marked on reverse. **$375-$450**

Large Frauenschaft neck brooch, pinback, RZM-marked on reverse. **$75-$125**

Small Frauenschaft neck brooch, pinback, RZM-marked on reverse. **$75-$95**

Women's helper service enamel neck brooch, pinback. **$185-$250**

1933 Frauenschaft type 1 enamel membership pin, pinback. **$275-$350**

1933 Frauenschaft type 1 enamel membership pin variant, pinback. **$275-$350**

Frauenschaft type 2 leader's enamel membership pin, Kreis level, RZM-marked on reverse. **$225-$275**

Frauenschaft type 3 enamel membership pin, pinback, RZM-marked on reverse. **$75-$85**

Frauenschaft young girls organization membership enamel pin. **$150-$195**

Frauenwerk membership enamel pin, pinback, RZM-marked on reverse. **$75-$95**

Women's sports event tinnie. **$85-$100**

Mother and children donation fabric tinnie. **$45-$65**

Franken Frauenschaft event tinnie. **$85-$100**

ReichsLuftschutzBund (RLB)

Due to the devastation of the unsuspecting population caused by aerial bombing during World War I, the German Weimar Republic government in 1926 developed an air protection agency under the command of the air ministry, for the purpose of instructing the general public in the event of future air attacks. The first training of these voluntary members began by the *Stahlhelm* (paramilitary group of ex-soldiers), then later by the *Arbeitsdienst* (labor corps).

When the Nazi Party led the German people into "total war" – the concept that any military or civilian target became acceptable – the air raid protection agency expanded into three main sections. The first section was the *Reichsluftschutzbund* (RLB, National Air Protection), the original and largest group, with the majority of members being voluntary and whose task was to instruct the public in air raid safety. The second section was the *Sicherheits und Hilfsdienst* (SHD, Security and Assistance Service) formed in 1940 to assist in the movement of crowds during large air raid emergencies. The third was the *Luftschutz Warndienst* (LSW, Air Warning Service) set up to report the approach of enemy aircraft. In 1942 the *Luftschutzpolizei* (Air Protection Police) was formed from the SHD members and placed under direct control of the SS to help better control the movement of civilians during air raid emergencies.

In addition, there was the *Wasserstrassenluftschutz* (groups for the protection of waterways) and the *Werkluftschutz* (WLS, air raid guards for private factories).

Since members of the first RLB organizations were mostly voluntary, insignia was not readily available to members in the beginning. However, as the organizations evolved and the war became more evident, air protection insignia and accoutrements could be found all throughout the Reich.

Early RLB members typically did not wear uniforms, with the exception of high-ranking officers and officials appointed by the air administration or by Herman Goering directly. The first official uniforms and regulations did not come into effect until 1934.

Members wore stickpins or pinback membership pins to show their relationship to the organization. The first pattern of the enlisted membership pin consisted of a silver starburst with a blue enamel "RLB" and swastika across the center. Officers' pins were comprised of a 19mm diameter blue enamel circle with a miniature copy of the enlisted pin overlaid in the center. A second pattern of the membership pin, which was not popular with the members, featured a simplified silver starburst containing only a black enamel rotated swastika in the center.

While participating in training exercises or fieldwork, active members commonly wore gray coveralls with a cloth Luftschutz emblem sewn to the right breast. The Luftschutz national emblem consisted of outstretched feathered wings cradling a small oak leaf crest, overlaid by a rotated swastika at the base and a banner across the center bearing the word *"Luftschutz."*

Several different forms of helmet shells were used, such as the gladiator style, so named because of its resemblance to a Roman gladiator helmet; the police-style square dip helmet; and the heavier M35 beaded "combat" helmet. These helmets were painted either dark blue or black and contained an RLB insignia decal across the front. In addition, as the Nazi war machine conquered other countries, a variety of captured helmets were repainted and pressed into service to accommodate the growing RLB organization.

When in civilian clothing, members could wear a Luftschutz armband consisting of a sky blue background supporting the white RLB sunburst emblem with either the early or late sewn "RLB" insignia in the center.

Standard membership identification books consisted of the *Reichsluftschutzbund* ausweis, a membership ID book with general information and monthly dues stamps; the *Luftschutz Dienstbuch* containing service records for members of the SHD and LSW; and the *Werkluftschutzpass* factory guard ID book.

When officials wore uniforms, they were Luftwaffe-style tunics with dark lapels and lilac-colored piping and patches. These attractive uniforms were finished off with matching riding pants or slacks, black leather belts, over-the-shoulder cross straps, silver buckles with the RLB insignia embossed on the front, black boots or shoes, and the standard NSDAP armband. Officers utilized the Luftwaffe-type peaked visor caps with the RLB insignia attached to the front above the brim. The insignia consisted of an upper silver metal or bullion right-facing eagle with one outstretched and one folded wing, standing on a starburst overlaid with a rotated black swastika, and a lower insignia of outstretched flat wings surrounding an oak leaf wreath encircling a roundel containing the red, white, and black national colors.

Uniformed RLB officers and later officers of subgroups were allowed to wear dress daggers and swords. The beautiful RLB dagger came in both officer and subordinate grades with a large two-sided polished blade, dark blue leather covering on the handle and scabbard, nickel silver pommel, and crossguard in the shape of a highly stylized straight-winged eagle with swastika. The handle of each contained a facsimile of the membership pins; earlier models bear the blue enamel RLB over sunburst design and later models bear the simpler silver sunburst with black enamel swastika. An official sword was not designated for the RLB, but because they were permitted for wear during formal occasions, lion's-head, dove's-head, and custom-made RLB swords were crafted for individuals to wear.

Members of the SHD and the LSW served in full-time capacities in lieu of military service and wore standard Luftwaffe uniforms with collar tabs bearing either stylized "SHD" or "LSW" on each side. Both groups wore the Luftschutz national cloth or bullion emblem attached to the right breast or left sleeve of their tunics. Specialties could be indicated by wearing qualification patches, such as the stylized "F" for fire control members, or armbands designating technical abilities, such as a red cross on white field for medical personnel. Ranking similar to the armed forces was indicated through the use of shoulder straps with pips, lace edging, and colored underlayment.

Officers utilized the Luftwaffe peaked visor cap, substituting the Luftschutz national emblem on top over a national cockade mounted on the cap band. Luftschutz helmets were used by members for protection when in the field. Standard RLB daggers were worn for dress occasions.

In 1942 the SHD was reorganized into the *Luftschutzpolizei* to better control the population during the increasing number of air raids affecting the countryside. Uniformed members substituted the German police emblem – spread-wing eagle standing on a rotated swastika surrounded by an oak leaf wreath – on cap fronts and left sleeves of their tunics.

WLS guards in factories wore gray Luftwaffe-style uniforms and gray overseas caps with the WLS cockade. The cockade insignia contained a right-facing, closed-winged eagle standing on a rotated swastika with a "W" and an "L" on either side. The eagle and swastika were encircled by an oak leaf wreath. As WLS guards worked in private factories, insignia and decals with company names or logos were often unofficially added to their helmets and uniforms.

The small waterway air raid protection group wore a variety of captured French uniforms with the addition of their insignia. This consisted of outstretched straight wings holding a vertical anchor overlaid with a circular oak leaf wreath surrounding a rotated swastika. The same emblem was also worn on the front of their overseas caps.

As Allied bombing missions pounded the military forces and general population of Germany into submission, members of the air protection league steadfastly carried out their duties and attempted to help both civilians and members of the armed forces avoid the increasing onslaught of destruction. RLB members skirted the hazardous piles of debris and burning asphalt streets of places like Dresden to pull the living and the dead from the cellars below. Because of their valiant efforts to save their fellow citizens from the destruction of Hitler's war, untold numbers of civilians survived to rebuild the free Germany of today.

RLB light-gauge beaded helmet with liner and decal. **$250-$325**

RLB first pattern leader's armband. **$185-$250**

RLB printed armband. **$150-$175**

RLB square dip police-type helmet with markings inside indicating ownership by a guard at the Mercedes Benz factory. **$675-$850**

RLB officer's tunic. **$1,000-$1,400**
(JAG)

SHD security and assistance service armband. **$150-$175**

(Private Collection)

RLB armband with acceptance stamp. **$165-$225**

SHD security and assistance service collar tabs. **$175-$225**

(Private Collection)

RLB quality-embroidered breast device. **$75-$85**

RLB heavy-gauge beaded helmet with liner and decal. **$375-$475**

Air raid factory guard armband. **$65-$80**

RLB standard woven breast device. **$45-$55**

RLB first pattern enlisted belt buckle, belt, and cross strap. **$350-$425**

RLB second pattern enlisted belt buckle. **$150-$185**

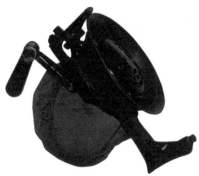

Vehicle siren with 1940 marked canvas cover, Bakelite upper frame, and crank handle. **$285-$325**

RLB equipment tag. **$45-$60**

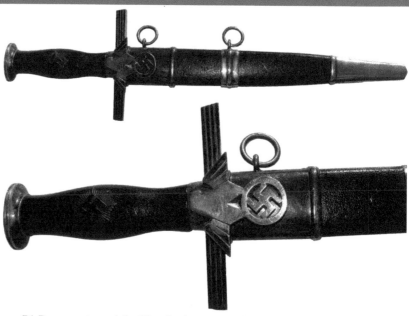

RLB second model officer's dagger, maker-marked. **$1,250-$1,500**

Factory-made custom saber with first RLB insignia riveted to the languet, maker-marked. **$800-$1,000**

RLB leader door plaque with enamel lettering. **$275-$325**

RLB members door plaque. **$175-$225**

RLB block leader ausweis. **$85-$100**

Booklet of RLB procedures. **$55-$75**
(Private Collection)

RLB service member's book. **$50-$65**

RLB second class service medal. **$145-$185**

RLB medal ribbon bar. **$25-$35**

RLB second model cap eagle with prongs. **$75-$95**

RLB first pattern visor cap badge, enamel lettering. **$85-$125**

RLB second pattern simplified visor cap badge with enamel swastika and prongs. **$75-$85**

RLB second pattern simplified badge with enamel swastika. **$45-$65**

RLB first pattern officer's badge with enamel lettering and border. **$125-$145**

RLB first pattern air spotter's membership pin, maker-marked. **$175-$225**

RLB first pattern large-scale membership pin with enamel lettering. **$85-$125**

RLB second model membership pin with enamel lettering. **$75-$95**

RLB second pattern air spotter's membership pin, maker-marked with serial number on reverse. **$185-$235**

RLB first pattern small-scale membership pin with enamel lettering. **$75-$95**

RLB donation event tinnie. **$65-$80**

RLB first pattern officer's badge stickpin with enamel lettering and border. **$125-$145**

RLB first pattern membership stickpin with enamel lettering. **$85-$100**

Deutsches Rotes Kreuz (DRK)

The *Deutsches Rotes Kreuz* (DRK, German Red Cross) had existed prior to World War I but received recognition as an official national organization through the Agreement of Geneva in 1929. After Adolf Hitler's ascension to power, the group was further legitimized by becoming a branch of the NSDAP (Nazi party) in 1937.

The DRK's standard regulations were published in 1938, and the organization experienced a period of rapid growth. The main goal of the group was the physical care of all citizens and soldiers of the nation, whether in peace or at war. Members included doctors, nurses, and assistants as well as a vast number of support personnel consisting of drivers, administration members, clerical workers, and others. Though the majority of members were volunteers, many professionals became full-time members as the war hastened the need for more medical care of both soldiers and civilians.

Volunteer members of the DRK typically wore membership pins to show their affiliation with the organization while off-duty. Membership pins went through four changes from 1934 to 1939. The first type featured small, 17mm enamel pins with a red cross over a white field surrounded by a silver boarder with the words *"Deutsches Rotes Kreuz"* in black around the outside. At the base was a swastika poised on point.

The second type was introduced in 1935 and consisted of an oval, 17mm by 22mm enamel pin with a black eagle over a red cross on a white field surrounded by a silver border with the same Red Cross lettering. The swastika was moved from the bottom border to the chest of the eagle.

The third edition introduced in 1936 consisted of a cutout eagle with rounded, down-sloped wings perched on a bright red enamel cross. A swastika balanced on end in a silver square was centered on the eagle's chest and there was no lettering.

The final version was introduced in 1939 and was similar to the third design, but with the wing shape altered from a gentle down-slope to a squared-off shape and elongated to reach down to either side of a supporting red cross.

Badges came in both stickpin and pinback versions. Many were marked with the maker's mark and *"Ges. Gesch"* (patent applied for), but none had the RZM mark as the DRK did not come under RZM control.

Registered nurses wore unique enamel badges at the neck closures of their uniforms. These consisted of a round 32mm badge with a black eagle with a silver-surrounded black swastika on its chest and perched on a red cross. The eagle sat on a white field, which in turn was surrounded by a colored border containing the words *"Deutsches Rotes Kreuz – Schwesternschaft."* The outer border color was determined by the wearer's rank: red for floor nurse, black for ward master, blue for supervisor, and green for division heads.

The reverse of each pinback badge had a makers' mark and a stamped serial number designating the recipient. Nurses were able to acquire a variant private-purchase oval badge, 30mm by 44mm, with the same design and colors as the standard issue round version. Nursing helpers wore a round 30mm badge with a red enamel cross on a white background surrounded by a black border with the words, *"Deutsches Rotes Kreuz Helferin"* and two swastikas. Senior helpers qualifying for long-term excellent service had the addition of a silver Greek key-design border added to their badges. Unskilled volunteers wore a round 28mm badge consisting of a red cross over white field surrounded by a black border with *"Deutsches Rotes Kreuz Samariterin"* and a swastika on the base.

Full-time male DRK personnel wore a uniform consisting of a gray wool tunic, matching pants, black boots, white or gray shirt, black tie, and a black belt (with or without cross strap) with silver buckle. Collar patches were gray (or brown for officers) to which were affixed red enamel crosses. Doctors wore their crosses mounted higher on the collar with a caduceus below. Ranking was indicated by a series of shoulder boards with various stripes, pips, and braiding. Since the DRK did not award decorations for long service, a series of silver stripes were worn on the tunic sleeves to designate years of service instead.

Beginning in 1938, a 105mm by 55mm triangular embroidered patch was worn on the right tunic sleeve. The patch featured an eagle perched on a round wreath surrounding a rotated swastika under which was printed the region and group of the member. Officers' patches were often constructed of silver bullion thread.

The uniform was topped off with a gray peaked visor cap with black visor and DRK emblem over an oak leaf wreath surrounding a roundel of national colors. An overseas cap typically worn in fieldwork was made of gray wool with a DRK emblem on the side and a roundel and stripe on the front. Armbands were only worn while on active duty and consisted of a variety of designs with the typical construction being a red cross surrounded by *"Deutsches Rotes Kreuz"* in black on a white field. Specialties, district names, and other details were added to the armbands to convey information about the wearer.

Lower-ranking women's uniforms consisted of a gray blouse with white skirt and apron, district patch on the right sleeve, and DRK armband. Ranking was designated by a series of colored pips on the collar tips. Officers wore gray blouses with dark gray skirts, black ties, sleeve patches, armbands, and black shoes. A service tunic similar to the one worn by males was worn along with a dark gray greatcoat. Nurses wore stiff white caps with either DRK repeated in a stripe around the rim, or a red cross predominantly displayed on the front. A dark gray fedora cap with a DRK cloth emblem sewn to the side brim was worn with the dress uniform.

Members of the DRK carried an 85mm by 120mm DRK *ausweis* (identification document). This folded white stock document had *"Perssonal Ausweis,"* the DRK emblem, and the area in which the member lived printed on the front cover. It opened to reveal a corner stamped and signed photograph of the member along with information about the individual, such as name, rank, level of expertise, birthdate, and address. The bottom of the page contained a yearly qualification stamp.

Members of the Red Cross were not supposed to carry weapons by virtue of their neutral roles –though some did in combat zones – but officers and enlisted men did carry specialized daggers. Enlisted DRK daggers consisted of a heavy-bladed hewer with a blunted tip

and serrated spine. The matt nickel-plated crossguard was of a plain, straight design with an oval on the front containing the DRK eagle and swastika in relief. The rear crossguard contained a plain oval on which some members engraved their initials or unit numbers. Two black plastic handles – checkered only on one side – were attached above the crossguard with screws that were topped off with a large funnel-shaped pommel. The hewer was carried in a black-painted steel scabbard with nickel-plated throat cap and toe, which in turn was mounted in a oversized black leather frog that could be attached to the enlisted man's belt. Though having a massive utilitarian appearance, DRK hewer frames and handles were somewhat fragile and would break with rough use.

Officers' daggers were constructed of a high polish double-edged blade with a smaller rendition of the hewer crossguard and pommel. The handle of the officer's model was made of round ribbed yellow or white plastic. The scabbard was of stippled nickel-plated steel with smooth toe design and two incorporated suspension rings. The dagger was suspended from a double hanger of silver and red cloth topped with dull aluminum oval buckles and clips.

Since the 1920s the Red Cross had bestowed a variety of badges and medals to members for excelling in service to the organization, but in 1939 Hitler abolished these awards. Instead, he ordered future DRK recipients receive social welfare awards, representing a more encompassing group that had multiple civic organizations. Higher forms of social welfare crosses and other badges were awarded mostly to military officers or preferred political heads of state. A more universally awarded decoration was the 30mm social welfare medal. This matt silver-colored round medal had a silhouette of the red cross eagle, swastika, and cross on one side, and *"Meddaille fur deutsche Volkspflege"* (medal for social welfare) on the reverse. The medal was suspended from a straight (for males) or bow-style (for females) red and white ribbon.

As the war across Europe continued to ravage the military and civilian population of Germany and its allies, DRK members were forced into increasingly perilous situations on the growing war front. Thousands died trying to save their own fellow citizens, who proved to be some of the most numerous victims of the Nazi war machine.

DRK enlisted visor cap. **$475-$550**

DRK enamel crosses on gray collar tabs, unissued attached set. **$85-$100**

1938 RDK tunic sectional id triangles. **$85-$125**

DRK officer's visor cap. **$575-$675**

DRK universal armband. **$45-$65**

DRK 1935 pattern sleeve eagle. **$65-$100**

(Private Collection)

DRK armband. **$75-$100**

DRK Bremen section tunic with musician's wings. **$750-$950**

DRK sports vest emblem. **$75-$85**

DRK enlisted belt buckle. **$275-$325**

DRK enlisted hewer with frog. **$775-$950**

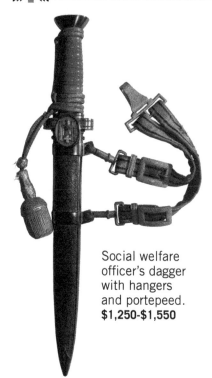

Social welfare officer's dagger with hangers and portepeed. **$1,250-$1,550**

DRK photos. **$5-$10**

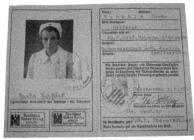

Ausweis for DRK low-level female member. **$85-$100**

Social welfare membership ausweis and record book. **$85-$125**

Social welfare ribbon for females, miniature version without pin. **$35-$45**

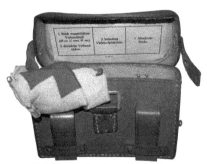

DRK medical pouch with armband. **$125-$145**

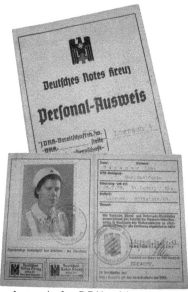

Ausweis for DRK mid-range female member. **$95-$125**

Social welfare medal for females, miniature version with pin. **$95-$125**

DRK soft-cover manual for first aid. **$65-$85**

DRK hard-bound manual for first aid with additional flyers. **$85-$95**

Three-place civilian mounted medal bar with iron cross, Hindenburg, and social welfare medals. **$300-$375**

(Private Collection)

Social welfare medal for females, full-size version with bow and pin. **$175-$195**

DRK type 3 senior helper's badge, pinback. **$175-$225**

DRK type 2 helper's badge, pinback. **$75-$95**

Midwife honor badge, 800 silver-marked wreath, pinback. **$575-$750**

Social welfare pinback membership pin. **$30-$45**

DRK type 4 unissued cap badge. **$65-$85**

DRK type 3 enamel membership badge, pinback. **$65-$85**

DRK type 2 enamel membership badge, pinback. **$85-$100**

DRK type 1 enamel membership badge, pinback. **$85-$100**

DRK nurse's badge, variant pinback style, serial numbered on reverse. **$300-$375**

DRK large type 4 enamel membership pin, pinback. **$65-$85**

DRK small type 4 enamel membership pin, pinback. **$55-$75**

Six-place medal stickpin with Imperial, Nazi, and social welfare medals. **$85-$125**

Social welfare stickpin for mother and child donation drive. **$65-$75**

DRK contribution stickpin on amber backing. **$75-$95**

DRK type 4 enamel membership stickpin. **$55-$75**

Other Groups

As the final goal was the undisputed control of citizens in all sections of the country, millions of Germans either volunteered or were coerced into joining many different trade, professional, paramilitary, or social groups in Adolf Hitler's regime. Besides the major organizations, many ancillary and specialty groups were either transformed or combined from those existing prior to the Nazi takeover, or started anew under the strict supervision of the Fascist government.

These groups could vary from national organizations with thousands of active members with diverse backgrounds to small specific professional groups with only a few regular participants. At their meetings, members would come together to share in their common interests, and at the same time, become further indoctrinated with the concepts of the Nazi party. It was not uncommon for German citizens to belong to multiple groups simultaneously, keeping their personal time (and non-conforming thoughts) to a minimum.

A sampling of the many organizations included:

Nationalsozialistischer Deutscher Studentenbund, NSDStB (N S German student league), started in 1926. College-age students' league for Nazi indoctrination. Emblem was an elongated swastika in a red and white diamond.

Reichskulturkammer, RKK (national culture organization), started in 1933. Organization of artists, authors, actors, and other providers of the arts and entertainment with many sub-groups formed by specialty. Founded to control all aspects of the arts. Emblem was an eagle over a swastika with the letters "RKK" underneath.

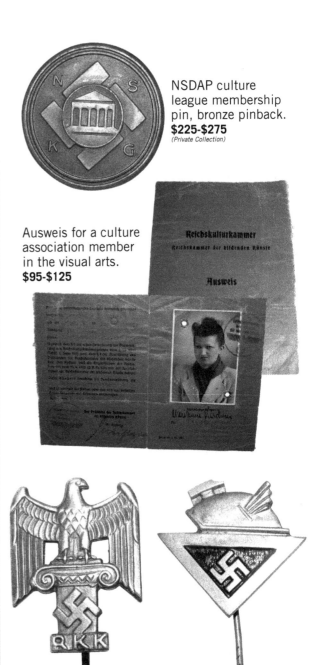

NSDAP culture league membership pin, bronze pinback. **$225-$275**
(Private Collection)

Ausweis for a culture association member in the visual arts. **$95-$125**

National culture organization membership stickpin. **$95-$125**

Confederation for German culture membership stickpin, maker-marked. **$85-$100**

Technische Nothilfe, Teno (technical emergency service), started in 1919. Large organization of technicians used in emergencies to restore public utilities, etc. Emblem was a rotated swastika overlaid by a gear surrounding a hammer-like "T" over an "N."

Teno membership pin, serial numbered on reverse. **$225-$275**

Teno officers collar patch set, metal on cloth backing. **$225-$285**

Organisation Todt, OT (engineering and construction organization), named after Fritz Todt and started in 1933. Large construction group used for public works and military installations. Main emblem was the letters "OT" with or without a geared swastika.

Reichspost (German postal service), started in 1495. National postal service. Main emblem was the national eagle, wreath, and swastika with the word *"Reichspost."*

Teno aluminum eagle with prongs for visor cap. **$75-$95**

Female postal worker beret. **$375-$450**

Teno trumpet banner, fringed with black reverse. **$525-$650**

Postal service unissued visor cap. **$475-$550**

Occupied Poland (general government) postage stamps. **$5-$10**

Postal tunic, unissued with 1939 dated paper tag in liner. **$575-$675**

Post office bank book set to one individual. **$125-$175**

Four Adolf Hitler postage stamps. **$5-$10**

Reichspost postal service armband. **$175-$225**

Reichspost postal service arm patch. **$65-$85**

Assorted postage stamps for the Reich. **$5-$10**

Reichspost auweis for workers. **$85-$135**

Nationalsozialistische Volkswohlfahrt, NSV (welfare organization), started in 1933. Provided food, clothing, shelter, and other aid to the poor, handicapped, and other "Aryans" not able to help themselves. Emblem was a circle containing the *Eif-Rune* (rune letter resembling a horizontal "Z") over a "V" and an "S."

Nationalsozialistische Kriegsopferversorgung, **NSKOV** (NS War Victims Welfare), started in 1934. Established to help disabled war veterans. Emblem was a wreath containing an upturned sword under a Maltese cross with a canted swastika.

NSKOV soldier families benevolent organization cap badge, 1937-1940 (facing right), with prongs. **$75-$95**

Wreath and roundel for postal visor cap. **$20-$25**

Post office eagle and wreath with prongs for visor cap. **$50-$65**

NSKOV soldier families benevolent organization cap badge, 1940-1945 (facing left), with prongs. **$75-$95**

Reichskolonialbund, RKB (German colonies association), started in 1936. Promoted the Nazi doctrines in past imperial colonial areas. Emblem was a cross-divided shield with one section having a red background and silver stars, the center of the cross overlaid with a canted black swastika.

German colonies association membership honor pin, enamel pinback. **$150-$185**

German colonies association membership honor enamel stickpin. **$150-$185**

German colonies association membership enamel pin. **$95-$135**

Volksbund Fur Das Deutschtum Im Ausland, VDA (association for Germans in foreign countries), started in 1881. Indoctrinated and politically used Germans outside of the Reich. Emblem incorporated a swastika and the letters "VDA."

Association for Germans living in foreign countries enamel membership pin. **$95-$135**

Deutscher Reichsbund Fur Leibesubungen, DRL (German national physical fitness group), started in 1934. Promoted countrywide athletic programs. Emblem was a square closed-wing eagle with a canted swastika on its chest.

National sports association sporting vest eagle. **$55-$75**

National sports association high-quality sports vest patch. **$250-$325**

National sports association winner's ribbon. **$100-$150**

Gymnastics association belt buckle. **$95-$150**

1936 Olympics souvenir cigarette case. **$275-$350**

1936 Olympics souvenir HJ knife with issue paper cover. **$1,200-$1,500**

1936 Olympics silver-plated top glass ink container. **$475-$650**

1936 Olympics souvenir silver spoon. **$175-$250**

National sports association tape measure. **$325-$450**

1936 Olympics silver goblet with ink stamp base. **$750-$1,000**

National sports association membership ausweis and record book. **$75-$95**

Early national sports association bronze award badge. **$75-$95**

Membership booklet for a national sports association member. **$65-$95**

National sports association miniature award pin in bronze. **$65-$85**

National sports association membership pin. **$65-$85**

National sports association miniature award pin in silver. **$65-$85**

1936 Olympics medal for workers and contributors. **$95-$150**

National sports association award pin in bronze. **$150-$185**

German gymnastics club event tinnie. **$125-$175**
(Private Collection)

1936 Olympics souvenir enamel pin. **$100-$135**

Early national sports association award stickpin. **$45-$65**

National sports association membership stickpin. **$65-$85**

Deutsche Lebensrettungsgesellschaft, DLRG (national lifesaving league), started in 1913. Volunteers for the promotion of safer swimming and lifeguard activities. Emblem was an eagle with the letters "DLRG."

German lifesaving membership ausweis for a Hitler Youth member. **$75-$90**

1934 Danzig gymnastics event stickpin, amber backing. **$175-$225**
(Private Collection)

1934 Nuremburg German games stickpin. **$125-$150**
(Private Collection)

National lifesaving league member swimsuit patch. **$35-$50**

Printed Volkssturm armband with sewn edges. **$65-$85**

Organization for families with many children pin, enamel, maker-marked. **$95-$135**

National lifesaving league membership pin. **$35-$55**

Organization for families with many children variant pin, enamel, maker-marked. **$95-$135**

Reichshebammenschaft (German midwives association), started in 1885. Specialized group teaching the skills needed for successful childbirth and childcare. Emblem was a white cross containing a relief of a mother and child, with "D," "R," "H," and a swastika on the cross arms.

Deutsches Siedlerbund, DSB (German homeowners association), started in 1933. Promoted home ownership under the Nazi regime. Emblem was a round winged eagle with "DSB" across its chest, covering a small house and slanted swastika.

Deutscher Volkssturm (German people's militia), started in 1944. A last-ditch assembly of elderly people, young teenagers, and other civilians to fight alongside the besieged German armed forces at the end of the war. Emblem was the national eagle, wreath, and swastika next to the words *"Deutscher Volkssturm Wehrmacht"* typically worn on armbands.

Reichsbund Der Kinderreichen, RDK (national union of large families), started in 1922. Promoted and assisted large families after the loss of life during World War I. Emblem was an eagle under "RDK" covering small chicks above a rotated swastika.

German homeowners association membership enamel pin. **$85-$125**

Reichsbundes Deutscher Kleingartner (small gardeners association). A pre-Nazi group that promoted growing and harvesting techniques by owners of small gardens. Emblem was a closed-wing eagle with a swastika on its chest surrounded by the organization's name.

German automobile club membership vehicle pennant. **$250-$350**

Small gardeners association enamel membership pin. **$65-$85**

German automobile club membership lapel pin, enamel. **$75-$95**

German automobile club 1934 honor stickpin, maker-marked. **$125-$150**

Small gardeners association 20-year honor enamel pin. **$175-$250**

Der Deutsche Automobil Club, DDAC (German automobile club), started in 1911. A national club that promoted driving and automobiles. Emblem was a down-winged eagle with "DDAC" on its chest perched on a red circle with white field and black swastika.

German automobile club membership sports vest patch. **$55-$75**

Guide map for the German automobile club. **$85-$125**

Deutscher Radfahrer Verband, DRV (German bicycle association), started in 1933. National club made up of older regional organizations to promote bicycling among enthusiasts. Emblem was a bicycle wheel overlaid with a swastika and the letters "DRV."

Bicycle association enamel membership stickpin. **$85-$125**

Deutscher Sangerbund (German Singers League), started in 1908. An organized union of professional singers. Emblem was a treble clef with a "D" and "B" on either side.

Berlin singing association embroidered patch. **$175-$195**

German Singers League metal and cloth membership stickpin. **$25-$35**

German Singers League honor enamel pin. **$45-$65**

National singing association honor stickpin. **$125-$150**
(Private Collection)

Deutsche Jagerschaft, DJ (association of German hunters), started in the 18th century. For the promotion and control of hunters and field practices. Emblem was a stag skull with upraised antlers surrounding a sunburst with a canted swastika in the middle.

Silver and black thread German hunting association membership patch. **$250-$325**

Bullion German hunting association membership patch. **$325-$425**

Early or pre-Nazi hunting association unit standard. **$675-$850**
(Chris Depere)

Fifty-year commemorative pin for East Prussian hunting association. **$175-$275**

1937 honor pin for the hunting association. **$225-$275**
(Private Collection)

German hunting association membership stickpin. **$75-$100**

Hunting horn with German hunting association emblem and hanger/tassel. **$385-$425**

German hunting license. **$55-$75**

German hunting association membership pin. **$150-$225**

With the final days of the Third Reich quickly approaching, many of these groups were abandoned as ordinary Germans turned their attention from the normal activities of their peacetime lives to the business of warfare and survival. After Germany's final defeat in the spring of 1945, all remaining groups either totally disbanded at the direction of the occupying Allies or reverted back to their pre-wartime organizations. The late 1940s and beyond saw the resurgence of many peacetime national German groups untainted by the evils of Adolf Hitler and the Nazi Regime.

Forestry official's shoulder boards. **$75-$95**

Forestry official's visor cap. **$650-$850**

Government service armband, department stamped. **$135-$150**

Reichsautozaug propaganda department vehicle patch. **$375-$475**

Forestry official's unissued work tunic with paper tag on liner. **$675-$825**

Munich visitor's souvenir patch. **$95-$125**

Forestry official leader's dress belt buckle with brocade belt. **$325-$450**

Forestry official leader's field belt and buckle, Assman-marked on reverse. **$225-$285**

German forestry official's senior's cutlass. **$1,200-$1,450**

National forestry official's deluxe subordinate's cutlass. **$950-$1,200**

EINGANG VERBOTEN

Auer Berlin

"Entrance Forbidden" enamel building sign. **$355-$400**

Gau-marked street donation can. **$135-$185**

1942 Berlin city dog license tag. **$35-$50**

"Strength through Joy" cruise ship souvenir cap tallies. **$175-$225**

Germany/ Saar region patriotic door decoration, maker-marked on reverse. **$165-$200**

Souvenir cigarette case for Hitler and Mussolini formal visit. **$225-$275**

Dutch Nazi party two-sided membership pennant. **$450-$600**

Porcelain 50th birthday Hitler table medal in issue box. **$250-$325**

GI-constructed "bring back": small party flag with RAD, police, Luftschutz, HJ, SS, and army patches roughly sewn on. **$450-$550**

Membership ausweis for the Czech South German party, precursor to the Nazi party in Czechoslovakia. **$75-$100**

Winter relief donation decorative paper slips. **$10-$15**

Winter relief glass suncatchers. **$25-$35**

Winter relief miniature book, *Struggle in France.* **$20-$35**

Winter relief Teutonic ax, sword, and shield with regional stones. **$20-$35**

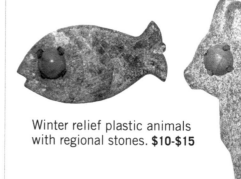

Winter relief plastic animals with regional stones. **$10-$15**

Winter relief plastic soldier on horseback and ship. **$20-$35**

Winter relief miniature songbook. **$20-$35**

Winter relief decorative
Christmas paper slips. **$10-$15**

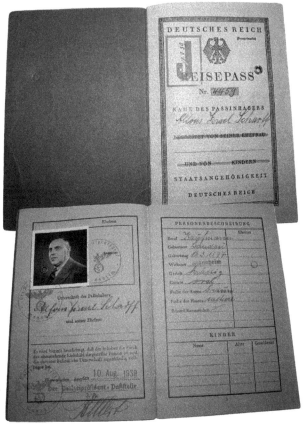

German passport for Jewish man, red "J"
stamped and "Israel" added as his middle
name. Entries show that he immigrated to
the United States. **$450-$650**

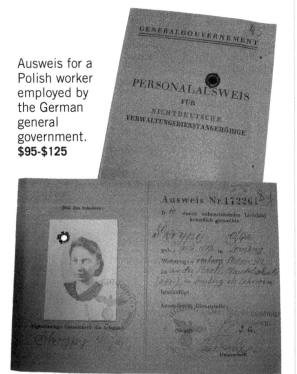

Ausweis for a
Polish worker
employed by
the German
general
government.
$95-$125

Lufthansa airlines
traveler's calendar
and fact book.
$75-$90

Reich's finance administration seals. **$20-$25**

Two different subscription payment books for newspapers. **$75-$95**

1939 health insurance document. **$10-$15**

1938 Reich's party day souvenir postcard. **$35-$50**

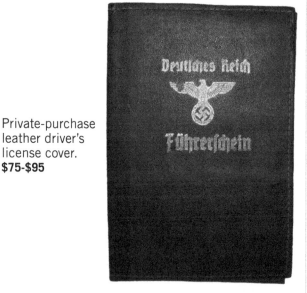

Private-purchase leather driver's license cover. **$75-$95**

Munich NSDAP souvenir picture book. **$45-$65**

Nuremburg complete souvenir postcard sets in holders. **$45-$65**

Propaganda book for the Czech/German takeover. **$35-$45**

Propaganda booklet for the German workers association. **$35-$55**

1943 souvenir picture book of German art. **$75-$100**

Certificate for giving warm clothing to soldiers on the front lines. **$45-$55**

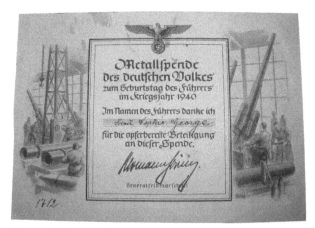

Recognition certificate for donating metal to the war cause during Hitler's birthday. **$45-$55**

Gold honor cross for the German mother (recognition for eight or more children). **$75-$95**

Gold honor cross, variant clipback, for the German mother. **$125-$145**

Photo of child in helmet with sword. **$10-$15**

Gold German mother's cross of honor in issue case with miniature award. **$275-$325**

Gold miniature honor cross with bow ribbon and pin for the German mother. **$85-$125**

Silver miniature honor cross with bow ribbon and pin for the German mother. **$85-$125**

Bronze miniature honor cross with bow ribbon and pin for the German mother. **$65-$85**

1943 enamel shooting award badge. **$75-$100**

NSDAP donation collection member badge, Gau-marked on reverse. **$175-$225**

1938 Nuremburg rally press pass badge, pinback. **$475-$650**

Silver honor cross for the German mother (recognition for six to seven children). **$75-$95**

Bronze honor cross for the German mother (recognition for four to five children). **$50-$75**

Horse rider's badge, bronze pinback, maker-marked reverse. **$150-$250**

Horse rider's badge, silver pinback, maker-marked reverse. **$250-$450**

General government eagle for visor cap. **$275-$325**

Thüringen guild local association pin with prongs. **$95-$125**

Silver horseman's badge, miniature pinback. **$150-$185**

Factory air raid guard cap emblem with prongs. **$150-$185**

Austrian Nazi party enamel/old silver membership badge. **$250-$325**

Winter relief enamel pinback donation pin. **$125-$150**

Political aluminum eagle and wreath with prongs. **$50-$75**

Thüringen guild local association pin with wreath. **$95-$125**

Winter relief porcelain donation pins, waiter and postal worker. **$35-$45**

Police donation pins, painted metal street signs. **$10-$25**

Winter relief cloth and tin regional donation pins. **$20-$35**

German people's Christian church membership pin. **$325-$400**

German Christian membership pin, painted, pinback. **$65-$85**

German Christians association membership pin. **$325-$400**

Lufthansa employees membership lapel pin, serial numbered on reverse. **$275-$325**

Organization of Eastern Germans membership enamel pin. **$75-$100**

Zeppelin shipping company enamel pin. **$175-$225**
(Private Collection)

Uniform button for a member of the zeppelin service. **$250-$300**
(Private Collection)

Runic plastic event tinnie, maker-marked on reverse, pinback. **$20-$30**

1937 wood and paint tinnie. **$75-$90**

(Private Collection)

1938 Nuremburg rally copper preferred seating tinnie. **$75-$90**

1938 Nuremburg rally standard event tinnie. **$35-$40**

1938 Nazi Kreis-level event tinnie. **$25-$35**

Munich visitor's souvenir stickpin, 800 marked. **$95-$125**

Germany/Saar region patriotic stickpin. **$65-$85**

Winter relief plastic on metal stickpin. **$25-$35**

German horse driver's badge in bronze, stickpin. **$75-$100**

Czech South German party wooden patriotic stickpin, 1938. **$75-$95**

Organization of
Eastern Germans
15-year honor
stickpin, enamel.
$175-$225

First class war
merit service cross
without swords
stickpin on issue
tag. **$75-$125**

Czech South
German
party enamel
membership
stickpin.
$85-$100

German war cemetery
keepers association
stickpin, pressed
painted tin. **$35-$50**

Civil defense
membership
stickpin.
$95-$135
(Private Collection)

Political event
lithographed
stickpin. **$35-$45**

National rifle target
shooters league
membership enamel
stickpin. **$75-$125**

Dutch Nazi party
membership
enamel stickpin.
$125-$175

Reproductions, Fakes, and Fantasy Pieces

An ongoing blight of Third Reich collecting over the past 70 years is the proliferation of reproductions, fakes, and fantasy pieces passed off as legitimate collectibles to unsuspecting buyers.

Unfortunately, this problem is not unique to German memorabilia. Any antique or collectible that commands a high selling price can fall victim to dishonest or uninformed dealers who want to make a quick buck. To combat this problem, savvy collectors have learned to use all available resources to educate themselves about a major purchase *before* making it. Authoritative reference books and websites combined with information acquired from primary sources, such as longtime collectors and veterans, will definitely shed light on what is a worthwhile item and what is one to avoid.

Reproductions are post-war items created to somewhat match the originals but are not designed specifically to fool buyers. Some collectors like reproductions because they fill a void in their collections when originals are too difficult or expensive to acquire.

Fakes are post-period items made to resemble the originals, and are sold as such to deceive collectors. They are often artificially aged and distressed to give the appearance of being period pieces.

Fantasy pieces are Third Reich-like pieces that never existed in the period. They can vary in appearance as to whatever the originator thinks will capture the imagination of a prospective customer and sell best in the current market – the flashier and more exotic, the better.

Evaluate Authenticity

Before purchasing an item for your collection, evaluate its authenticity. First, consider the item's dimensions. If a medal is supposed to be 30mm across,

be sure to measure it. Not every piece will be exact, due to minute manufacturing variances or surface wear, but the measurement should be reasonably close. Some reference books show actual size images that can be directly compared to an item. In the past, some European manufacturers of reproductions deviated their sizes slightly to circumvent the legal complications of being liable for producing deceptive fakes.

The next things to look at are markings and the reverse surface. Many advanced collectors will study the reverse side of a collectible, like a badge, more than the front side. Maker's markings, "patent applied for" lettering (*Ges Gesch, Gesetzlich geschutzt*), and RZM marks (*Reichszeugmeisterei*), if applicable, are important though not conclusive. Marks were stamped or cast onto some badges and awards, but not on all – especially those produced later in the war – which makes their presence or absence not always a deciding factor in originality. Reverse metal oxidation, pin or stickpin attachment (if appropriate), and general wear should also be considered when studying the back of an item. Keep this in mind: The German military – Heer, Kriegsmarine, and Luftwaffe – was not controlled by the RZM authorities, so its badges, awards, and equipment will not have RZM marks.

Color is the next item of study. Fabric dyes used during the Third Reich did not always stand up well to the test of time, and colors can be faded. Some more modern hues of cloth and paint were not used on legitimate Third Reich collectibles, so matching colors to various Third Reich groups will help determine if they are correct for the period or not. It's easy to spot new leather compared to old leather – new leather is much brighter and won't show 70 years' worth of grime and wear as old leather will.

Patina or surface oxidation is a good indicator of an item's age, though artificial aging can be achieved with the use of modern chemicals. Where patina exists, such as on a dagger handle, look for wear patterns and handling marks. If oxidation is spread evenly over an entire surface, it may have been chemically applied recently rather than occurring naturally over a long period of time.

Construction, Fit, and Finish

Studying the correct construction, fit, and finish of Third Reich items takes a fair amount of effort, but it pays off in the long run. For example, knowing that 2nd class period iron crosses are made of iron, brass, or alloy cores with two silver-plated or silver frames soldered around the outsides can prevent a collector from buying an often-faked modern piece. Daggers are particularly susceptible to reproduction and fakery due to their high values. Poorly fitting pieces, bad machining on blades and outside surfaces, and inadequately plated finishes are giveaways for modern copies. The same poor quality can be seen in modern copies of higher-priced badges and awards of the Third Reich.

Knowing which materials were used for period items is of great worth. Many synthetic fabrics are not 70 years old, so a silk-screened Third Reich banner made from synthetics is a good indication it is of recent origin. Plastic-handled SA daggers, painted rather than leather-covered scabbard coverings, plastic helmet headliners, brass-framed dagger handles, and many other examples can be spotted as modern fakes when a collector learns what is correct for the period.

Recognizing the approximate weight of item will help as well. If an item is typically made of steel but feels like aluminum or another lightweight alloy metal when held, there is a chance it may be not correct for the period.

Odors are difficult to fake or reproduce. After 70 or 80 years, old cloth flags, paperwork, and uniforms typically will have a musty smell, regardless of how well they have been stored. Old leather looks and smells like old leather with none of the acidic scent of new leather.

Unfortunately, personality pieces are regularly faked and put on the market. Newly created documents and personal items claiming to be from Hitler, Himmler, Hess, Goering, and several others are regularly sold as legitimate vintage pieces. Always research an item thoroughly before buying it.

Buying Tips

The Internet has become a marketing mecca for collectibles in the last 20 years. It can be a truly wonderful hunting ground, but also the proverbial minefield for both inexperienced and seasoned collectors. A buyer must trust a seller's ability to "see and feel" a piece to determine if it is original as stated. Photographs on a website may not always accurately represent an item's condition or originality. Therefore, it is important to know a seller before you buy from him. Check out his background and read reviews or comments about his products and selling practices. Purchase only from individuals who guarantee their items as period and who allow returns with full refunds.

The profusion of reproductions and fakes can cause some collectors to be overly wary of items from the Third Reich. In addition, the lack of supplies during World War II (Germans were thrifty in their use or repurposing of available materials) created some marked deviations between original pieces and textbook examples from the same period. But with conscientious effort, and by following a few basic steps, most collectors can enjoy a rewarding hobby with a minimum of exposure.

First, buy from the veteran who acquired the items or a relative of the veteran, if possible. Many times he may not know what the items are, though information has become more readily available. Prepare before meeting the seller.

Second, whether buying from a single dealer or a larger business, stick to reputable vendors who know what they have, present it accurately, and have a reasonable and stated return policy. This last point is a standard for trustworthy dealers. If an item is genuine and returned to them in the same condition as received, they should have no problem reselling it. Keep this in mind especially if purchasing from dealers on the Internet.

Finally, take the time and make the effort to research a collectible and perform due diligence before making a purchase. There are a number of excellent and highly detailed reference books available that deal with specific areas and groups of the Third Reich. Some people will study consumer reviews, magazine articles, and Internet blogs for hours before purchasing a $500 television, but then plunk down $1,000 without doing any research on an SS helmet based on unsubstantiated information. A huge part of collecting is studying the hobby, lessening the risk, and helping preserve history for future generations.

Bibliography

Angolia, LTC John R., *For Fuhrer and Fatherland: Military Awards of the Third Reich*, 3rd ed. San Jose, CA: R. James Bender Publishing, 1976.

Angolia, LTC John R., *For Fuhrer and Fatherland: Political & Civil Awards of the Third Reich*, 2nd ed. San Jose, CA: R. James Bender Publishing, 1978.

Angolia, LTC John R., *Cloth Insignia of the NSDAP and SA*, 1st ed. San Jose, CA: R. James Publishing, 1985.

Angolia, LTC John R., *In the Service of the Reich*, 1st ed. San Jose, CA: R. James Bender Publishing, 1995.

Angolia, LTC John R. and Littlejohn, David, *Labor Organizations of the Reich*, 1st ed. San Jose, CA: R. James Bender Publishing, 1999.

Angolia, LTC John R. and Littlejohn, David, *NSKK NSFK Uniforms, Organization & History*, 1st ed. San Jose, CA: R. James Bender Publishing, 1994.

Angolia, LTC John R. and Taylor, Hugh Page, *Uniforms, Organization & History of the German Police, Volume 1*, 1st ed. San Jose, CA: R. James Bender Publishing, 2004.

Angolia, LTC John R., *Belt Buckles and Brocades of the Third Reich*, 1st ed. San Jose, CA: R. James Bender Publishing, 1982.

Angolia, LTC John R. and Taylor, Hugh Page, *Uniforms, Organization & History of the German Police, Volume 2*, 1st ed. San Jose, CA: R. James Bender Publishing, 2009.

Angolia, LTC John R. and Schlicht, Adolf, *Uniforms & Traditions of the Luftwaffe, Volume 1*, 1st ed. San Jose, CA: R. James Bender Publishing, 1996.

Angolia, LTC John R. and Schlicht, Adolf, *Uniforms & Traditions of the Luftwaffe, Volume 2*, 1st ed. San Jose, CA: R. James Bender Publishing, 1997.

Angolia, LTC John R. and Schlicht, Adolf, *Uniforms & Traditions of the Luftwaffe, Volume 3*, 1st ed. San Jose, CA: R. James Bender Publishing, 1998.

Berrafato, Enzo and Berrafato, Laurent, *Kriegsmarine History Uniforms Headgear Insignia Equipment 1935-1945*, 3rd ed., Atglen, PA: Schiffer Publishing, Ltd., 2012.

Bowman, J.A., *Third Reich Daggers 1933-1945*, 1st ed., Livonia, NY: R & R Books, 1994.

Cone, J. R., *One People, One Reich: Enameled Organizational Badges of Germany 1918-1945*, 1st ed., Tulsa, OK, MCN Press.

Davis, Brian Leigh and Turner, Pierre, *German Uniforms of the Third Reich 1933-1945*, 5th ed., New York, Sterling Publishing Co., 1987.

Davis, Brian Leigh, *Badges & Insignia of the Third Reich 1933-1945*, 4th ed., New York, Sterling Publishing Co., 1994.

Hayden, Mark, *German Military Ribbon Bars 1914-1957*, 1st ed., Atglen, PA, Schiffer Publishing Ltd., 2001.

Hayes, Arthur and Maguire, Jon, *Uniforms of the Third Reich*, 1st ed. Atglen, PA, Schiffer Publishing Ltd., 1997.

Hayes, A., *SS Uniforms, Insignia & Accoutrements: A Study in Photographs*, 1st ed., Atglen, PA, Schiffer Publishing Ltd., 1996.

Krawczyk, Wade, *German Army Uniforms of World War II: In Color Photographs*, 1st ed., Osceola, WI, Motorbooks International Publishers and Wholesalers, 1995.

Lumsden, Robin, *SS Regalia*, 2nd ed., Edison, NJ, Chartwell Books, Inc., 1996.

Johnson, LTC Thomas M., *Collecting the Edged Weapons of the Third Reich, Volume 1*, 2nd ed., Columbia, SC, published by the author, 1977.

Littlejohn, David, *The Hitler Youth*, 1st ed., Columbia, SC, Agincourt Publishers, 1988.

Lyndhurst, Joe, *Military Collectibles: An International Directory of Twentieth-Century Militaria*, 1st ed., London, Salamander Books, Ltd., 1983.

Miller, David, *Fighting Men of World War II Axis Forces: Uniforms, Equipment & Weapons*, 2nd ed., New York, Chartwell Books, Inc., 2011.

Smith, Jill Halcomb and Saris, Wilhelm P.B.R., *Headgear of Hitler's Germany, Volume 1*, 1st ed., San Jose, CA: R. James Bender Publishing, 1989.

Smith, Jill Halcomb and Saris, Wilhelm P.B.R., *Headgear of Hitler's Germany, Volume 2*, 1st ed., San Jose, CA: R. James Bender Publishing, 1992.

Smith, Jill Halcomb and Saris, Wilhelm P.B.R., *Headgear of Hitler's Germany, Volume 3*, 1st ed., San Jose, CA: R. James Bender Publishing, 1998.

Stephens, F.J., *Hitler Youth: History Organisation Uniforms and Insignia*, 1st ed., Surrey, UK, Byron Press, Ltd., 1973.

Young, Jeffrey F. and Meinz, Daniel W., *German Third Reich Era Documents, Volume 1*, St. Joseph, MN, published by the authors, 1997.

Young, Jeffrey F. & Meinz, Daniel W., *German Third Reich Era Documents, Volume 2*, St. Joseph, MN, published by the authors, 1998.

Young, Jeffrey F. & Meinz, Daniel W., *German Third Reich Era Documents, Volume 3*, St. Joseph, MN, published by the authors, 2007.

Index

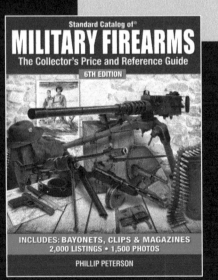
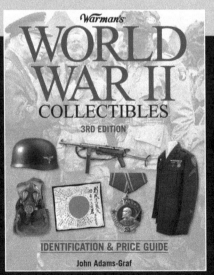
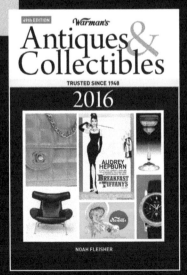